Frank H. Challis

Semi-centennial Compendium of historical Facts 1846

Business and political Index of Manchester, N.H.

Frank H. Challis

Semi-centennial Compendium of historical Facts 1846
Business and political Index of Manchester, N.H.

ISBN/EAN: 9783337143374

Printed in Europe, USA, Canada, Australia, Japan

Cover: Foto ©ninafisch / pixelio.de

More available books at **www.hansebooks.com**

Manchester Savings Bank, Cor. Elm and Market Sts.

1846
Semi-Centennial
Compendium
of
Historical Facts

Business and
Political Index of
Manchester, N.H.
1896

COPYRIGHTED 1896 BY FRANK H. CHALLIS.

Cor. Elm and Market Sts... Manchester Savings Bank

Boston & Maine Railroad.

SOUTHERN & WHITE MOUNTAIN DIVISION.

SUBJECT TO CHANGE.

TRAINS LEAVE MANCHESTER.

For Nashua, Lowell and Boston, 5.59, 6.19, 6.29, 8.05, 8.27, 10.50, 11.06 A. M., 3.03, 4.11, 5.31, 6.59 P. M. Sundays, 6.19, 6.29, 8.06 A. M., 4.55 P. M.

For Nashua and intermediate stations, 5.59, 8.27, 11.06 A. M., 4.11 P. M.

For Portsmouth and intermediate stations, 8.30, 11.10 A. M., 4.15 P. M.

Via Rockingham Junction for Portland, Dover, Rochester, Farmington and Exeter, 8.30 A. M., 4.15 P. M.

For stations on Manchester & North Weare Branch, Henniker and New Boston, 10.25 A. M., 5.05 P. M., Sundays, 3.10 P. M.

For Hooksett and Suncook, 5.25, 8.47, 10.15 A. M., 2.16, 4.55, 7.35, 9.37 P. M. Sundays, 4.10 A. M., 3.07, 7.05, 9.37 P. M.

For Hooksett and stations on Suncook Valley branch, 10.15 A. M., 4.55 P. M. Sundays, 7 05 P. M.

For Concord, 5.25, 8.47, 10.15, 10.41 A. M., 1.04, 2.16, 2.37, 4.55, 6.35, 7.35, 9.10, 9.37 P. M. Sundays, 4.10 A. M., 3.07, 7.05, 9.10, 9.37 P. M.

For way stations to Groveton, Fabyan's, Gorham and Berlin, 10.41 A. M. Change cars at Concord.

For Tilton, Laconia, Lakeport, Meredith, Ashland, Plymouth, Woodsville, Bath, Lisbon, Littleton, Lancaster, Groveton, 10.41 A. M., 2.37 P. M.

For Tilton, Laconia, Lakeport, Meredith, Ashland, Plymouth, Rumney and local stations to Woodsville, 10.41 A. M., 2.37, 9.37 P. M.

For Plymouth and stations on Pemigewasset Valley branch, 10.41 A. M., 2.37 P. M.

For Belmont, 2.37 P. M.

For Plymouth and local stations south of Plymouth, 10.41 A. M., 2.37, 6.35 P. M.

For Passumpsic Division, via Plymouth, 10.41 A. M., 2.37, 9.37 P. M.

For stations on Montpelier & Wells River R. R., 10.41 A. M., 2.37 P. M.

For St. Paul and Western points, via "Soo Line." 10.41 A. M.

For Chicago and Western points, 10.41 A. M., 9.37 P. M.   (9.37 P. M., train runs daily, including Sundays.)

For Chicago and all Western points, via White River Junction, 1.04 P. M.

TRAINS LEAVE BOSTON, UNION STATION, CAUSEWAY STREET,

For Manchester, 6.40, 8.30, 9.00, 11.30 A. M., 12.00, 1.00, 3.00, 5.00, 5.25, 7.30, 8.00 P. M. Sundays, 2.00 A. M., 1.00, 5.00, 7.30, 8.00 P. M.

[Time Table Western and Concord Divisions, Page 31.]

MANCHESTER ELECTRIC LIGHT CO.

People's Gas Light Co.

2

1896 JANUARY 1896

SUN.	MON.	TUE.	WED.	THU.	FRI.	SAT.
Last Quarter 7th	New Moon 14th	First Quarter 22nd	1	2	3	4
5	6	7	8	9	10	11
12	13	14	15	16	17	18
19	20	21	22	23	24	25
26	27	28	29	30	31	Full Moon 30th

HISTORICAL COMPENDIUM.

Abbot, Theodore T., mayor 1855, 1856, 1863, died in Lunenburg, Mass., March 30, 1887, aged 88.

Abbott, William O., book canvasser, soldier, etc., died Jan. 26, 1895, aged 64.

Abels, Charles, Print Works overseer, died April 19, 1892.

Accident, railroad, at Hooksett, July 30, 1887. Express Messenger French and Brakeman Barney killed.

Accident, bridge, at Hooksett, Dec. 19, 1888. Middle bridge fell, three men drowned.

Act defining duties of firewards in certain cases (Portsmouth act of Dec. 16, 1828) adopted for Manchester, Oct. 26, 1839.

Adams, Phinehas, elected agent Stark mills, Nov. 6, 1847, died July 23, 1883, aged 69.

Aldrich, Charles, once principal of the Intermediate school, died Sept. 12, 1887, aged 80.

Almy, Frank C., murderer, hanged at Concord, May 16, 1893.

American Mechanics, Order of United, grand parade in honor of the National Council, Sept. 26, 1892.

Amoskeag Bridge Company formed in 1792, and "McGregor's bridge" built.

Amoskeag Cotton and Woolen Manufacturing Co. incorporated June, 1810, succeeding "The Proprietors of the Amoskeag Cotton and Wool Factory" which was organized Jan. 31, 1810.

Amoskeag Manufacturing Company incorporated 1831.

Andrew, B. S., elected principal of Webster-street school, March 29, 1889.

Ankarloo, John P., one of earliest Swedish residents, died May 21, 1894, aged 71.

Anniversary, one hundredth, of town celebrated Oct. 22, 1851. Address by Rev. C. W. Wallace, poem by William Stark.

4

1896 FEBRUARY 1896

SUN.	MON.	TUE.	WED.	THU.	FRI.	SAT.
Last Quarter 5th	New Moon 13th	First Quarter 21st	Full Moon 28th			1
2	3	4	5	6	7	8
9	10	11	12	13	14	15
16	17	18	19	20	21	22
23	24	25	26	27	28	29

HISTORICAL COMPENDIUM — Continued.

Anniversary, 50th, of first newspaper celebrated Nov. 16, 1889.

Ancient Order Hibernians:
   Division 1, organized 1874.
   Division 2, organized November, 1880.

Anniversary, silver, of Knights of Pythias of state, celebrated Oct. 15, 1895.

Ancient Order of United Workmen:
   Pioneer Lodge, No. 1, instituted July 31, 1878.
   Security Lodge, No. 8, instituted April 20, 1883.

Appropriation for preaching and schooling voted in March, 1784, and town divided into four school districts.

Association, Granite State Provident, chartered 1881; charter amended 1887; organized Dec. 5, 1887; began business 1888; assets, about $3,000,000.

Arcanum, Royal, Delta Council, No. 84, organized May 8, 1878.

Association, Excelsior Literary, famous debating society, organized Jan. 4, 1858.

Association, Manchester Art, organized September, 1871, incorporated Oct. 13, 1874, rooms 45 Pickering building.

Association, Manchester Building and Loan, organized Jan. 11, 1887.

Association, Maine, formed March 4, 1895.

Association, Vermont, organized Feb. 3, 1888.

Association, Young Men's Christian, formed March 3, 1854, disbanded March 3, 1862; rejuvenated April 13, 1868, and again became defunct about 10 years thereafter; reorganized Nov. 15, 1893; rooms in Pembroke block.

Association, Young Woman's Christian, formed Sept. 23, 1872; rooms in basement of Franklin-street church.

1896 MARCH 1896

SUN.	MON.	TUE.	WED.	THU.	FRI.	SAT.
1	2	3	4	5	6	7
8	9	10	11	12	13	14
15	16	17	18	19	20	21
22	23	24	25	26	27	28
29	30	31	Last Quarter 6th	New Moon 14th	First Quarter 22nd	Full Moon 29th

HISTORICAL COMPENDIUM — *Continued.*

Athenaeum, Manchester, organized 1844. Afterwards merged in city library.

Aubin, Rev. Gideon, ordained over French Protestant church, March 24, 1881.

Aurora Borealis, wonderful display, Jan. 5, 1892.

Austin, Col. Hiram, old resident, died April 4, 1886, aged 80.

Austin, Jeremiah, manufacturer, died Feb. 20, 1892, aged 71.

Avery, Rev. N. A., resigned from Merrimack-street Baptist church, Dec. 15, 1894.

Bacheler, James S., machinist, old fireman and city official, died Nov. 22, 1892.

Bacon, Rev. F. S., called to Tabernacle Baptist church, Dec. 15, 1891.

Balch, Col. Chas. E., cashier Manchester bank, died Sept. 10, 1884, aged 50.

Balch, Capt. Daniel, property owner, died Aug. 22, 1875, aged 78.

Baldwin, Fred C., resigned from Ash-street school, July 7, 1893.

Baldwin, Deacon James, bobbin manufacturer, died May 22, 1893, aged 81.

Bank, Amoskeag, state, organized for business October, 1848; succeeded by Amoskeag National, organized Nov. 1, 1864. Capital $200,000.

Bank, Amoskeag National, opened safety vaults, March 11, 1893.

Bank, Amoskeag Savings, chartered June 19, 1852.

Bank, City, chartered by state, July 2, 1853; now Merchants National Bank.

Bank, City Savings, chartered June 25, 1859; suspended 1877.

Bank, Commonwealth National, organized Jan. 30, 1892; suspended July 24, 1893.

7

Photographs ✒ on Albumen Paper

We use Albumen Paper because it is the best, and because
many of the best Photographers will use no other.
You are invited to call and examine our work and learn
why we do not use enameled paper unless it is ordered.

⚜

Studio -- 780 Elm St.   **J. T. LANGLEY**

GEO. W. PETTIGREW,
Wig Maker and Hair Worker

. . . .

HAIR GOODS SPECIALTIES.

. . . .

120 Bridge Street,   -   -   Manchester, N. H.

ALWAYS ON HAND
FINE STOCK OF CUT FLOWERS

J. RAY. BROOK.
GARDENS Co.

Floral Designs

At Short Notice.

▾▾

OFFICE :

30 Hanover Street.

GREENHOUSES :

969 Union Street.

Brault's Digestive Elixir

IS A SURE CURE FOR

Dyspepsia in All Its Forms.

ALL DRUGGISTS SELL IT

8

1896 *APRIL* 1896

SUN.	MON.	TUE.	WED.	THU.	FRI.	SAT.
Last Quarter 4th	New Moon 13th	First Quarter 20th	1	2	3	4
5	6	7	8	9	10	11
12	13	14	15	16	17	18
19	20	21	22	23	24	25
26	27	28	29	30		Full Moon 27th

HISTORICAL COMPENDIUM — *Continued.*

Bank, Derryfield Savings, suspended July 24, 1893.

Bank, Manchester, chartered December, 1844, organized 1845, ceased business in 1866.

Bank, Manchester National, organized April, 1865, to succeed the Manchester Bank.   Capital $150,000.

Bank, Manchester Savings, chartered July 8, 1846.

Bank, Mechanics Savings, organized Dec. 1, 1877.

Bank, Merrimack River, chartered July 14, 1855, name changed to First National 1865.

Bank, Merrimack River Savings.   See Institution, Five Cents Savings.

Bank of New England, closed its doors July 24, 1893; resumed business Jan. 15, 1894.

Bank, Peoples Savings, organized August, 1875; began business Oct. 1.

Barnard, Marden E., dry-goods man, drowned in Massabesic, Aug. 23, 1887, aged 39.

Barr, Deacon Ira, 25 years grocer, died May 29, 1888, aged 72.

Barry, Alderman Richard J., appointed plumbing inspector April 6, 1894.

Bartlett, Ezra W., real estate owner, died Feb. 26, 1879, aged 66.

Batchelder, Betsey, died Sept. 14, 1879, aged 93.

Bean, John D., clothing dealer, died Aug. 17, 1890, aged 70.

" Bell Mill," second mill in Manchester, and also another mill on the island in the river, built 1826.

1896   MAY   1896

Sun.	Mon.	Tue.	Wed.	Thu.	Fri.	Sat.
Last Quarter 4th	New Moon 12th	First Quarter 20th	Full Moon 26th		1	2
3	4	5	6	7	8	9
10	11	12	13	14	15	16
17	18	19	20	21	22	23
24/31	25	26	27	28	29	30

HISTORICAL COMPENDIUM — *Continued.*

Bell, Hon. Samuel N., financier, ex-congressman, died Feb. 8, 1889, aged almost 60.

Bennett, Winfred H., elected city engineer Jan. 5, 1886.

Berry, William H., assistant secretary N. H. Fire Insurance Co., died Aug. 12, 1894, aged 61.

Blanchard, John, murdered Sept. 30, 1880, by Pierce F. Powers, who was sent to state prison for five years.

Block, Dunlap, completed Oct. 21, 1879.

Block, Morris, sold to Amoskeag bank, at rate of $40 per foot, July 2, 1892.

Blodget, Hon. Samuel, born in Woburn, Mass., April 1, 1724. He became a sutler during the colonial war and the Revolution, judge of court of common pleas, and merchant. Became a resident of Derryfield, near Amoskeag falls, in 1793.

Blodget, Hon. Samuel, began work on canal around Amoskeag falls May 2, 1794. Lost his fortune in enterprise and raised much money by lotteries. Canal completed May 1, 1807.

Blodget, Hon. Samuel, died September, 1807. His monument in the Valley cemetery describes him as "the pioneer of internal improvements in New Hampshire."

Blood, Aretas, presented Bartlett place worth $25,000 to Women's Aid and Relief Society, Jan. 14, 1892.

Blunt, Gen. Asa P., distinguished soldier, died Oct. 4, 1889, aged 62.

Boiler explosion, at Lowell's iron foundry, May 5, 1889.

Boothby, Dentist Willard M., with Mrs. Geo. Kennem, disappeared Jan. 18, 1889, a noted sensation.

11

12

1896 *JUNE* 1896

SUN.	MON.	TUE.	WED.	THU.	FRI.	SAT.
	1	2	3	4	5	6
7	8	9	10	11	12	13
14	15	16	17	18	19	20
21	22	23	24	25	26	27
28	29	30				

Last Quarter 3d   New Moon 11th   First Quarter 18th   Full Moon 25th

HISTORICAL COMPENDIUM — *Continued.*

Borthwick, Rev. M. W., called to First Christian church, April 22, 1894.

Bradford, Capt. J. L., died Feb. 19, 1882, aged 69.

Bradley, Rt. Rev. Dennis M., appointed bishop April 11, 1884, consecrated June 11, 1884. Went on a European trip, 1887, and received grand return reception, Nov. 15.

Bragg, Rev. L. D., appointed pastor of St. James M. E. church, Sept. 10, 1892.

Bridge, Amoskeag Falls, built 1842. Cost $12,069; carried away by freshet 1852; rebuilt 1852.

Bridge, Granite, built 1840; carried away in 1851, and rebuilt same year.

Bridge, first in Manchester, built across Cohas brook, 1738.

Bridge, McGregor, first built 1792, became worthless about 1815, replaced 1825, partially destroyed 1848, entirely carried away 1851; rebuilt of iron in 1881 and opened Aug. 12. Cost about $100,000.

Bridge, Piscataquog, built 1843; burned 1862; replaced by iron bridge same year and fell under a loaded team 1873; wooden bridge replaced it and stone bridge succeeded that in 1894.

Bridge, Second-street, iron, built 1893. Cost $50,000.

Bridge, North Weare railroad, burned June 17, 1891.

Briggs, Mrs. Roxanna, wife of Hon. J. F. Briggs, died Jan. 27, 1888, aged 63.

Brooks, George W., 47 years in Amoskeag mills, died Aug. 16, 1894, aged 75.

Brooks, Rev. Nahum, died March 17, 1883, aged 72.

Brown, Hiram, Whig, elected first mayor, Sept. 1, 1846, at a second election, receiving 602 votes against 552.

14

1896 JULY 1896

SUN.	MON.	TUE.	WED.	THU.	FRI.	SAT.
Last Quarter 2nd	New Moon 10th	First Quarter 17th	1	2	3	4
5	6	7	8	9	10	11
12	13	14	15	16	17	18
19	20	21	22	23	24	25
26	27	28	29	30	31	Full Moon 24th

HISTORICAL COMPENDIUM — *Continued.*

Brown, Sylvester, elected master of Squog school, Jan. 2, 1875.

Buck, William E., elected superintendent of schools, April 6, 1877.

Building, government, corner-stone laid May 25, 1888.

Building and Loan Asso., Manchester, organized May 18, 1887.

Building, Union, corner Elm and Market streets, first erected by private parties on west side of Elm street, built by Ayer & Leach, 1841. Occupied first by E. W. Harrington who had previously occupied first building built upon Elm street.

Buncher, Mrs. Mary J., former city librarian, army nurse, died in Nashua, July 10, 1895, aged 73.

Bunton, Dr. Sylvanus, died Aug. 13, 1884, aged 72.

Burgess, Alpheus C., real estate owner, 46 years a resident, died April 17, 1889, aged 73.

Burpee, Col. Benj. P., died Nov. 1, 1888, aged 70.

Cadets, Manchester, organized June, 1873.

Campbell, James M., formerly editor of Union, died April 30, 1883, aged 65.

Canal, upper, is 5480 feet long; lower, 6900 feet.

Canney, Dr. H. C., died April 21, 1893, aged 54.

Carley, Etta J., school teacher, died Feb. 14, 1890, aged 34.

Carlsson, Rev. Carl, called to Swedish Lutheran church, June 21, 1894. Installed Oct. 26.

Lunch Tongue and all Picnic Specialties at Manchester Tea Store.

15

1896 *AUGUST* 1896

SUN.	MON.	TUE.	WED.	THU.	FRI.	SAT.
Last Quarter 1st–31st	New Moon 9th	First Quarter 15th	Full Moon 23rd	☞	☞	1
2	3	4	5	6	7	8
9	10	11	12	13	14	15
16	17	18	19	20	21	22
23/30	24/31	25	26	27	28	29

HISTORICAL COMPENDIUM — *Continued.*

Carpenter, Calvin D., veteran sexton, died July 25, 1895, aged 75.

Carter, Rev. C. F., resigned from South Main-street church, Jan. 11, 1886.

Cathedral, St. Joseph's, consecrated April 15, 1894.

Challis, Abigail L., 46 years mill operative, started first dresser in No. 3 Amoskeag, died January, 1890.

Challis, Major Timothy W., prominent veteran, past department commander G. A. R., ex-alderman, president of common council, died Feb. 1, 1890, aged 62.

Chamberlin, Henry Rust, city treasurer many years, died Aug. 16, 1881, aged—

Chandler, Adam, father of the Chandler brothers, bankers, died Sept. 6, 1887, aged 82.

Chandler, Deacon P. K., died Nov. 10, 1886, aged 63.

Chapel, Methodist, Hallsville, dedicated April 13, 1888.

Chapel, Union, South Manchester, dedicated May 14, 1893.

Chase, Harvey, grocer, and 40 years a resident of Manchester, died Feb. 27, 1888, aged 60.

Chase, John B., tanner, 40 years resident in town, councilman and representative, died April 6, 1888, aged 73.

Chase, Stephen P., committed suicide, April 14, 1885, aged 64.

Cheney, Person C., elected governor by legislature, June 9, 1875; Cheney 193, Roberts 186.

Chesley, Deborah, committed suicide by hanging, June 25, 1888, aged 82.

WILLEY'S BOOK OF NUTFIELD

And Semi-Centennial History of Manchester.

HON. HENRY W. BLAIR,

ex-United States Senator, says:

We have nothing in the line of local or even state history which at all approaches it in attractiveness of general appearance, nor in comprehensive as well as minute historic value. Mr. Willey's plan seems to be to seek out everything and to preserve what is best worth preserving in the past, while presenting a complete photograph of the present, so that the whole will become an acknowledged authority for future times. I think that the "Book of Nutfield" will be one of permanent value and of great interest to thousands in all parts of the country.   (Signed)   HENRY W. BLAIR.

1896 SEPTEMBER 1896

Sun.	Mon.	Tue.	Wed.	Thu.	Fri.	Sat.
New Moon 7th	First Quarter 13th	1	2	3	4	5
6	7	8	9	10	11	12
13	14	15	16	17	18	19
20	21	22	23	24	25	26
27	28	29	30		Full Moon 21st	Last Quarter 29th

HISTORICAL COMPENDIUM — *Continued.*

Children, 700, entertained at Massabesic by ex-Gov. Fred'k Smyth, July 7, 1891.

Chimney, big Amoskeag, completed June, 1893; height 265 feet.

Choate, Rev. Washington, installed over Franklin-street church Sept. 30, 1875; resigned Nov. 25, 1876.

Church, "pew ground" sold in church at the Centre, 1790; price payable two-thirds in "glass, nailes or marchantable clabboards or putty," and the balance in cash.

Church, Bethel Advent, organized Aug. 8, 1870, though Advent services were held as early as 1843.   Church built on Amherst street, 1894.

Church, first organized in Manchester, was of the Baptist denomination, formed in 1812 by David Abbott and 13 others.   It dissolved after existing several years.

Church, First Baptist, organized 1839, built first church at corner of Manchester and Chestnut streets, 1840; burned in 1870.   Present church corner of Concord and Union streets, dedicated April 30, 1873.

Church, Free Will Baptist, built 1841.

Church, Merrimack-street Baptist, organized as Second Baptist church Oct. 31, 1845.   Bought second story of block corner Elm and Pleasant streets 1849.   Declined to pay for same and dedicated present house Oct. 27, 1857.

Church, Pine-street Free Will Baptist, formed Dec. 21, 1859.

Church, St. Raphael's Catholic, corner-stone laid Aug. 19, 1888.

Church, St. Joseph's Catholic, dedicated April 28, 1869.

19

1896 OCTOBER 1896

SUN.	MON.	TUE.	WED.	THU.	FRI.	SAT.
New Moon 6th	First Quarter 13th	Full Moon 21st	Last Quarter 29th	1	2	3
4	5	6	7	8	9	10
11	12	13	14	15	16	17
18	19	20	21	22	23	24
25	26	27	28	29	30	31

HISTORICAL COMPENDIUM — *Continued.*

Church, First Christian, formed Sept. 21, 1870; formally organized Jan. 15, 1871.

Church, Congregational, organized Dec. 2, 1828, in Amoskeag; in 1839 removed to the "new village," and became the first church to hold regular services there. United with Presbyterian church at the Centre Aug. 15, 1839, and became First Congregational church.

Church, new First Congregational, dedicated May 12, 1880.

Church, Franklin-street Congregational, organized June 27, 1844. Name adopted Dec. 17, 1847. Church dedicated Dec. 22, 1847. Society organized May 7, 1844. Rev. Henry M. Dexter first pastor. Church repaired 1878. Possesses chime of bells presented by ex-Gov. Smyth.

Church, Grace, Episcopal, organized as St. Michael's, Nov. 29, 1841. Name changed June 2, 1862. Church building consecrated Dec. 28, 1843. Replaced by present stone structure, consecrated Dec. 4, 1860.

Church, Grace, chapel opened Nov. 9, 1886.

Church, St. Michael's Episcopal, built corner Lowell and Pine streets, 1843. Society organized 1841.

Church, French Protestant, organized March 24, 1881.

Church, Methodist, First, organized at Centre Sept. 27, 1829. Its church was begun 1829 and completed 1830, the first built in Manchester.

Church, Second Methodist, organized Dec. 16, 1839, in the "new village."

Church, Second Methodist, built church corner Elm street and Dean avenue, 1842. Dedicated Dec. 6.

If your Grocer don't keep the article you want ask for it at the Tea Store.

21

1896 NOVEMBER 1896

SUN.	MON.	TUE.	WED.	THU.	FRI.	SAT.
1	2	3	4	5	6	7
8	9	10	11	12	13	14
15	16	17	18	19	20	21
22	23	24	25	26	27	28
29	30					

New Moon 5th   First Quarter 12th   Full Moon 20th   Last Quarter 27th

HISTORICAL COMPENDIUM — *Continued.*

Church, St. Paul's M. E., formed by union of the Second Methodist and the North Elm-street M. E. church, which had seceded in 1855, April 7, 1862. Present church corner-stone laid June 3, 1882; dedicated April 13, 1883; repaired 1895.

Church, Peoples M. E., dedicated Nov. 26, 1882.

Church, St. James M. E., dedicated April 19, 1892.

Church, Tabernacle M. E., organized by Rev. J. Benson Hamilton, May 2, 1878.

Church, First Wesleyan Methodist, formed March 13, 1849, dissolved about 1854.

Church, Presbyterian, formed at Manchester Centre, May 21, 1828. It never had a building or a pastor of its own. United with Amoskeag Congregational church Aug. 15, 1839.

Church, First Presbyterian, built November, 1820. In 1842 it was sold to " The Piscataquog Village Academy." Occupied by Wesleyan Methodists 1855. Church organized Nov. 9, 1859; dissolved Dec. 20, 1867. Building repaired and rededicated April 21, 1872. South Main-street Congregational church, organized 1883, occupies building.

Church, Second Presbyterian, organized Oct. 28, 1884.

Church, German Presbyterian, dedicated June 28, 1885.

Church, Westminster Presbyterian, dedicated Dec. 6, 1892.

Church, Swedish Lutheran, corner-stone laid Oct. 9, 1886.

1896 DECEMBER 1896

SUN.	MON.	TUE.	WED.	THU.	FRI.	SAT.
New Moon 4th	First Quarter 11th	1	2	3	4	5
6	7	8	9	10	11	12
13	14	15	16	17	18	19
20	21	22	23	24	25	26
27	28	29	30	31	Full Moon 19th	Last Quarter 27th

HISTORICAL COMPENDIUM — *Continued.*

Church, Unitarian, preliminary meeting, April 24, 1842; constitution adopted April 27; church organized July 19; given lot corner Merrimack and Pine streets, 1843; swapped this with First F. W. Baptist society, corner Chestnut and Merrimack, 1859; sold this 1871 and built present house 1872.

Church, Lowell-street Universalist. B. M. Tillotson, pastor; dedicated February, 1840. Cost $6,500; repaired 1878 and rededicated Oct. 11.

Cilley, Bradbury J., appointed postmaster 1865.

Cilley, Col. Bradbury P., died March 22, 1892, aged 68.

Cilley, Joseph, ex-U. S. senator, died in Nottingham, Sept. 16, 1887, aged 96.

City Government, first, organized Sept. 8, 1846, Moses Fellows presiding and Rev. C. W. Wallace offering prayer. Oath of office was administered to the mayor by Hon. Daniel Clark.

City hall lot voted to be bought for $2,500, Feb. 1, 1841, and $20,000 voted to erect building. John D. Kimball, Edward McQuesten and J. T. P. Hunt, committee. First building cost $17,000.

Clapp, Rev. T. Eaton, preached initial sermon at Hanover-street church, Feb. 4, 1894. Installed April 18.

Clark, Daniel, U. S. Judge and ex-U. S. senator, died Jan. 2, 1891, aged 81.

Clark, David J., appointed postmaster 1861.

Clarke, Mrs. John B., died May 10, 1885, aged 66.

Clarke, John B., editor of Mirror, died Oct. 29, 1891, aged 71.

Clark, Capt. Joseph B., ex-mayor, etc., ends his life by hanging, Oct. 22, 1886.

Clark, "Tim," former city hall janitor and noted character, accidentally burned to death, Oct. 12, 1894, aged 77.

20

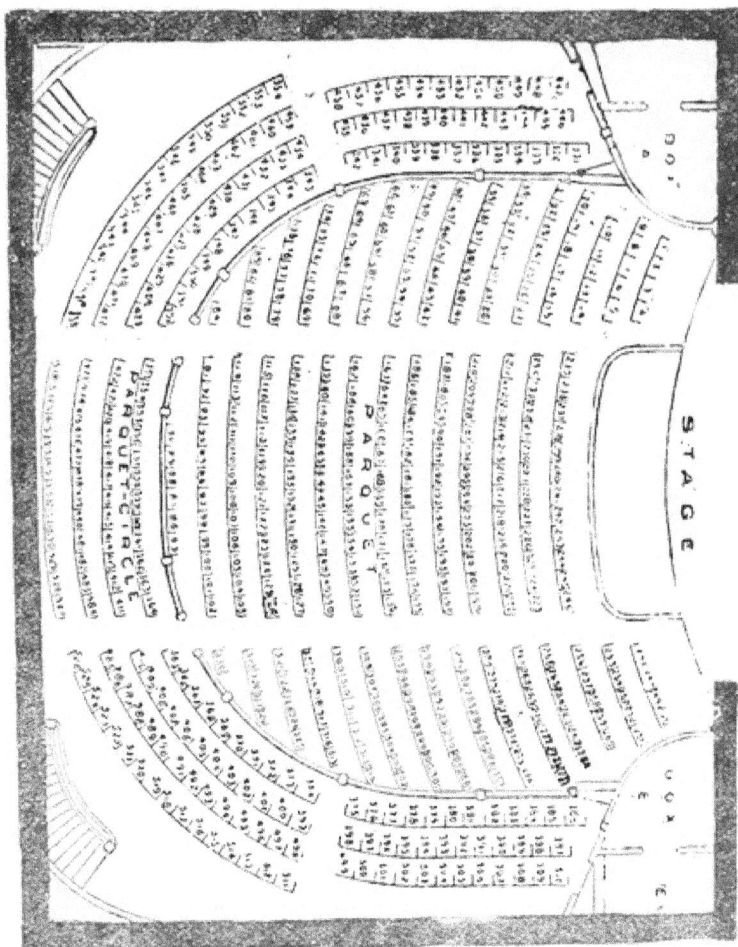

MANCHESTER OPERA HOUSE--PARQUET PLAN.
(BALCONY PLAN--PAGE 29.)

HISTORICAL COMPENDIUM — *Continued.*

Clarke, William C., elected mayor Nov. 6, 1894, by 932 plurality. Other city vote: Governor, Busiel, R., plurality 1485; congressman, Sulloway, R., plurality 1421; sheriff, Healey, R., plurality 405; senators—Gould, R., plurality 371; Woodbury, R., plurality 834; Bartlett, D., plurality 928.

Cleworth, John, reed manufacturer, died Jan. 16, 1887, aged 76.

Cleworth, Thomas, dyer in Manchester mills many years, died May 29, 1895, aged 72.

Clough, Lucien B., ex-probate court judge, died July 28, 1895, aged 72.

Club, Calumet, organized 1887; incorporated 1895; club house 126 Lowell street.

Club, Derryfield, organized April 13, 1875; club house 17 Mechanic street.

Club, Granite State, rooms opened in Pembroke block, Sept. 12, 1890.

Club, Jolliet, organized March 17, 1884; incorporated May, 1885; rooms, Upton block.

Club, Manchester Press, organized Dec. 3, 1892; rooms in "The Kennard."

Colby, Henry, 35 years watchman at Manchester mills, main gate, died Jan. 12, 1889, aged 60.

Colby, Rev. N. L., installed over Merrimack-street Baptist church, July 17, 1879.

28

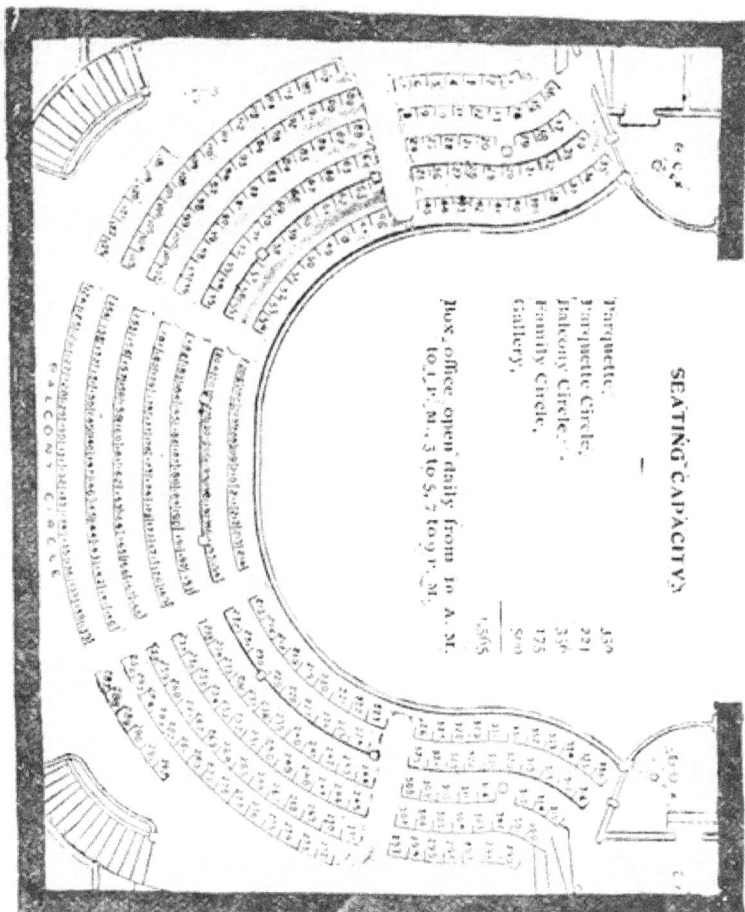

MANCHESTER OPERA HOUSE--BALCONY PLAN.

7-20-4

10-CENT CIGAR.

LITTLE GOLD DUST

Havana Filled 5-Cent Cigar.

R. G. SULLIVAN, Manufacturer,

MANCHESTER, N. H.

ALBERT MOULTON,

Manufacturer of New and Dealer in all Kinds of Second-Hand

BARRELS AND CASKS

28 to 50 Winter Street, - West Manchester, N. H.

BARRELS FOR SALE IN CAR LOAD LOTS, MORE OR LESS.

For Flour, Sugar, Meal, Coffee, Soda, Crackers, Spices, Etc., Etc. For Apples, Potatoes, Onions, Glauber Salt, Ground Bone, Ground Mica, Alum, Fertilizers, Shoe Heels, Twine, Pegs, Counters, Crockery, Glassware, Etc., Etc. For Liquor, Cider, Vinegar, Pork, Lard, Hams, Etc., Etc.

Highest cash price paid at all times for all kinds of second-hand barrels and casks, lard and butter tubs, tea mats, tea lead, etc.

REFERENCE: AMOSKEAG NATIONAL BANK.

HISTORICAL COMPENDIUM — *Continued.*

College, St. Anselem's Benedictine, burned Feb. 18, 1892; loss $60,000; rebuilt and dedicated Oct. 11, 1893.

Collins, David T., old time fireman, died March 9, 1891, aged 54.

Columbus, Knights of, Manchester Council No. 92, organized April 22, 1894.

Company, Amoskeag Mutual Fire Insurance, organized Dec. 24, 1840, did business for four or five years; revived 1860 and did business for a short time.

Company, Elliott Manufacturing, incorporated April, 1892; capital $150,000.

Company, Eureka Shoe, incorporated November, 1894; capital $50,000.

Company, S. C. Forsaith Machine, incorporated 1884; capital $275,000.

Company, Manchester Gas-Light, incorporated 1841; began business 1852; capital $100,000.

Company, Peoples Gas-Light, incorporated 1887; capital $300,000; operates works of Manchester Gas-Light Co.

Company, Gerrish Wool and Leather, incorporated January, 1891; capital $100,000.

Company, New Hampshire Fire, chartered 1869; first stock insurance company in the state.

Company, Manchester Rifle, organized 1825; disbanded 1848.

Company, Union Electric, incorporated 1893; capital, $150,000.

Cooke, Rev. Henry E., installed at Grace Church, March 28, 1886.

Cooper, Lt. Samuel, veteran, mechanical draughtsman, died Dec. 27, 1891, aged 58.

Commission, police, appointed Dec. 1, 1893. Members, Isaac L. Heath, Noah S. Clark, Frank P. Carpenter.

Committee appointed to petition legislature to change name of Derryfield to Manchester, March 13, 1810. Thomas Stickney, John G. Moor and Amos Weston, committee.

Connolly, Major Thomas J., gallant soldier, died March 22, 1888, aged 58.

Corliss, Horace D., 40 years a restaurateur and an employe of No. 1 Stark mill in 1840, died Feb. 26, 1888, aged 65.

Correction, house of, built on town farm, 1843.

Boston & Maine Railroad.

SUBJECT TO CHANGE.

WESTERN DIVISION.   MANCHESTER & LAWRENCE BRANCH.

FOR MANCHESTER, N. H.

Leave Boston 7.30 A. M., 12.25, 2.55, and 5.01 P. M., week days.   Sundays 8.00, 11.45, A. M., 6.00 P. M.

Leave Lawrence, 8.37 A. M., 1.18, 3.48, and 5.55 P. M., week days.   Sundays, 9.20 A. M., 12.58, 7.02 P. M.

Leave Windham, 9.04 A. M., 1.47, 4.08, and 6.25 P. M., week days.   Sundays, 9.48, A. M., 1.29, 7.38 P. M.

Leave Derry, 9.11 A. M., 1.56, 4.15, and 6.34 P. M., week days.   Sundays, 9.56 A. M., 1.39, 7.36 P. M.

FOR BOSTON.

Leave Manchester, N. H., 6.25, 8.05, 11.25 A. M., 4.35 P. M., week days. Sundays, 7.10 A. M., 4.45. 5.50 P. M.

Leave Derry, 6.51, 8.24, 11.50 A. M., 5.00 P. M., week days.   Sundays, 7.38 A. M., 5.00, 6.15 P. M.

Leave Windham, 7.00, 8.31, 11.58 A. M., 5.08 P. M., week days.   Sundays, 7.48 A. M., 5.08, 6.22 P. M.

Leave Salem, N. H., 7.11, 8.40 A. M., 12.09, 5.19 P. M., week days.   Sundays, 7.59 A. M., 5.19, 6.33 P. M.

CONCORD DIVISION.—Passenger Service from Manchester, N. H.

For Montreal and Central Vermont Railroad Stations, 10.41 A. M., 1.04, 9.10 P. M.

For Passumpsic Division Stations, 10.41 A. M., 1.04, 9.10 P. M.

For Franklin, Lebanon and White River Junction, (ex) 10.41 A. M., 1.04, 6.35, 9.10 P. M.

For White River Junction and Way Stations, 10.15 A. M., 6.35 P. M.   Sundays, 4.10 A. M.

For Bristol and Hill, 10.41 A. M., 2.37 P. M.

For Franklin and Way Stations south of Franklin, 2.37 P. M.

Through train for Quebec via White River Junction and Passumpsic Division at 10.41 A. M., 1.04, 9.10 P. M.

CLAREMONT BRANCH.

For Claremont Junction, Newport, N. H., Newbury, (Lake Sunapee) and Way Stations, 8.47 A. M., 2.37 P. M.

For Peterboro, Keene, Hancock Junction, Hillsboro' and Way Stations, 8.47 A. M., 2.37 P. M.

D. J. FLANDERS,	WM. F. BERRY,
Gen'l Pass. and Ticket Agt.	Gen'l Traffic Manager.

31

HISTORICAL COMPENDIUM — *Continued.*

Court-house, county, built 1868, cost $42,000. Land bought for city and county purposes in 1847.

Crandall, Horace, once driver of E. W. Harrington steamer, died March 13, 1895, aged 85.

Crane, Rev. E. C., installed at South Main-street Congregational church, April 14, 1886; resigned Dec. 8, 1889.

Crosby, Dr. Josiah, an eminent physician, died Jan. 7, 1875.

Crosby, Dr. Geo. A., eminent physician, died Jan. 30, 1888, aged 56.

Cross, Ira, elected mayor by 661 plurality, March 15, 1876.

Cumner, Benj. G., 27 years in clothing business, died Nov. 15, 1887, aged 54.

Cumner, Nathaniel W., former business man, mason, president of common council 1863, died in Boston Aug. 13, 1888.

Currier, Dea. Benj., died Sept. 7, 1887, aged 81.

Currier, Capt. Chas., 23 years Amoskeag overseer, died Sept. 26, 1880, aged 73.

Currier, Hon. Moody, resigned as president of Amoskeag bank; succeeded by Hon. Geo. B. Chandler.

Currier, Hon. Moody, inaugurated governor June 4, 1885. Elected November, 1884. Plurality in Manchester 409.

Cushman, Charles H., leading young business man, died Dec. 1, 1895, aged —

Dam, Amoskeag, built 1837, rebuilt 1871. Main dam is 420 feet long, wing dam 230 feet, height averages 12 feet, width at top eight feet, cost about $60,000; greatly damaged in freshet of 1894, and repaired at cost of $25,000.

Daughters of Liberty:
Molly Stark Council, No. 1, organized Sept. 6, 1890.
Lady Wentworth Council, No. —, organized Nov. 23, 1893.
Columbia Council, No. 20, organized Dec. 21, 1894.

Davis, Rev. W. V. W., installed pastor Franklin-street church, Sept. 12, 1877; resigned ——

Dean, Benj. C., resigned as superintendent print works, Oct. 26, 1891.

Dean, James, supt. Manchester print works, died Nov. 30, 1875, aged 57.

32

HISTORICAL COMPENDIUM — *Continued.*

Dearborn, Josiah G., appointed postmaster March 22, 1886.

Deed of 10 miles square in what was known as the "chestnut country," afterwards Nutfield, granted to Rev. John Wheelwright, Oct. 20, 1719.

Deer captured and killed on Merrimack common, Jan. 3, 1894.

Demarest, Rev. G. L., resigned from —— Feb. 1, 1875.

Democrat, Manchester, established May 3, 1842, by W. H. Kimball and Joseph Kidder.

Deposits, savings, received by Amoskeag Co., from 1842 to September, 1865. At that time it had $200,000 on deposit.

Derryfield, charter of, granted Sept. 3, 1751.

Derryfield classed with Litchfield for representative in 1793.

Dickey, Andrew J., ex-alderman, etc., died Dec. 12, 1892, aged 63.

Dickey, Henry C., veteran, watchman at print works many years, died Oct. 21, aged 58.

Dignam, Walter, leader of old Manchester Cornet Band, died April 22, 1891, aged 63.

Dillon, John J., resigned as colonel First Regiment, Aug. 4, 1881.

Dodge, Geo. W., nominated for convention by democrats, Sept. 15, 1886.

Dodge, James E., appointed city auditor, Jan. 26, 1894.

Dodge, Malachi F., mill superintendent, farmer, representative in legislature from Nashua, Londonderry and Manchester, died Dec. 10, 1888.

Dodge, Simon, colonel in old militia, ex-councilman, died Aug. 7, 1895, aged 75.

Donahoe, James T., clothing merchant, died June 17, 1895, aged 48.

Downs, Frank L., 10 years captain Manchester Cadets, resigned Sept. 3, 1895.

Drake, Amos P., 24 years employed by Gas Co., died Aug. 12, 1886, aged 61.

33

HISTORICAL COMPENDIUM — *Continued.*

Driving park, Manchester, sold at auction for $22,000, Jan. 26, 1895.

Dunham, William G. H., veteran and business man, died March 13, 1892, aged 48.

Dunlap, Thomas, veteran jeweler, died May 15, 1892, aged 69.

Dunn, Cyrus, 35 years a grocer, died Dec. 5, 1888, aged 72.

Durgin Charles A., 15 years Amoskeag overseer, died April 6, 1894, aged 61.

Durrell, Rev. J. M., resigned from St. Paul's church, April 17, 1891.

Earthquake, severe shock experienced May 1, 1891.

Eastman, Judge Ira A., died March 21, 1881, aged 72.

Egan, John F., elected captain of Emmet Guards, Dec. 29, 1894.

Electric Light Co., Ben Franklin, incorporated June 5, 1886. Operated by Peoples Gas-Light Co.

————, Manchester, chartered 1881; capital $80,000.

Elks, Order of, Manchester lodge, instituted Dec. 13, 1889.

Ellis, Nathaniel W., civil engineer, died in Boston, Jan. 16, 1889, aged 39.

Emerson, William, old resident, died May 8, 1887, aged 82.

Emery, Asa K., old resident and associate of Uncle John Maynard as a builder, died May 27, 1894, aged 78.

Engineer's office created Jan. 6, 1875.

Engine house, Gen. Stark, dedicated Dec. 27, 1888.

Engine house, Merrimack, dedicated Oct. 23, 1889.

Erhardt, Rev. Fred, installed over German Presbyterian church Oct. 10, 1882, resigned 1885.

Everett, Henry H., 20 years newspaper writer, died March 24, 1895, aged 53.

HISTORICAL COMPENDIUM — *Continued.*

Everett, Joseph, 40 years a resident, died Sept. 16, 1887, aged 81.

Fabens, Capt. Geo. O., died April 5, 1882, aged 50.

Falls, Amoskeag, have a height of 54 feet 10 inches.

Farmer, Daniel, old resident of Amoskeag, alderman, etc., died Aug. 7, 1890, aged 75.

Farmer, Daniel D., committed first known murder in town, Oct. 4, 1821, he killing a worthless woman of Goffstown named Anna Ayer, in a fit of passion. Was tried in October at Amherst, and hung Jan. 22, 1822.

Farmer, Peter, old resident, died Jan. 9, 1890, aged 73.

Farrington, Henry G., died April 11, 1883, aged 76.

Farrell, John A., prominent A. O. U. W. man, died Dec. 2, 1886.

Fife, Mary J., 20 years a school teacher, died June 26, 1888, aged 54.

Fire in basement of Music Hall block, loss $10,000, Sept. 22, 1886.

Fire on Cedar street, two women burned, Jan. 24, 1886.

Fire department, chief of, salary made $1,000 and elected for three years, Dec. 31, 1886.

Fire engine, first steam, bought 1859.

Fire in Frank P. Kimball's clothing store, biggest loss of the year, Dec. 29, 1891.

Fire Insurance Co., Peoples, organized Oct. 27, 1885, ceased business 1893.

Fire in Novelty Printing establishment, loss $8,000, Dec. 3, 1892.

Fire, March 16, 1850, burned portion of No. 2 Stark mill, loss $30,000.

Fire, July 5, 1852, burned Baldwin & Co.'s steam nail where Varney's brass works are, and several adjoining buildings.

Fire, Sept. 22, 1853, burned print works main building, loss $260,000.

35

HISTORICAL COMPENDIUM — *Continued.*

Fire, July 15, 1855, burned south half No. 1 print works mill, loss $270,000. Fire same time burned out all buildings where Merchants' Exchange stands, and most of the other buildings between Hanover, Chestnut, Manchester and Elm streets.

Fire, Feb. 5, 1856, burned Patten's block, destroying the city library, three newspaper offices, etc. Loss, $75,000.

Fire, July 8, 1870, burned over territory between Hanover, Chestnut, Manchester south back street and Elm east back street. Loss, $200,000.

Fire, at State Industrial School, Dec. 20, 1865, partially destroyed building. Inmates were housed in the "Stark house" and "Gamble house," till the former was burned and the school building repaired.

Fire wards, Amory Warren, Hiram Brown, David A. Bunton, Henry S. Whitney, John H. Maynard, William P. Farmer, Timothy J. Carter, James Wallace, Mace Moulton, George W. Tilden, Isaac N. Ford, elected Oct. 26, 1839.

Fire, disastrous, in Varick building, loss $144,000, Feb. 7, 1892.

Fire, Webster block, several persons suffocated, Aug. 7, 1885.

First city election was held Aug. 19, 1846. There were four candidates for mayor, Hiram Brown, William C. Clarke, Thomas Brown, and William Shepherd. Brown lacked 17 votes of an election. At a second trial Sept. 1, the candidates were Hiram Brown, Thomas Brown, Isaac C. Flanders, and John S. Wiggin. Hiram Brown was elected by 24 majority over the other three.

First land sale of Amoskeag Company, Oct. 24, 1838. One hundred and forty-seven lots sold between Elm, Lowell, Union and Hanover streets. Merrimack and Concord squares were reserved.

First mill of any kind was built in 1736 by Major Ephraim Hildreth, it being a saw mill on Cohas brook, then called Massabesic river.

L. B. BODWELL & CO.,

·· DEALERS IN ··

Coal, Wood and Ice

· · · · · · · · · ·

640 ELM ST., MANCHESTER, N. H.

L. B. BODWELL.   · ◆ ·   A. BODWELL.

HISTORICAL COMPENDIUM — *Continued.*

First mill built in Derryfield at Amoskeag in 1809, by Benjamin Prichard, Ephraim, David, and Robert Stevens.

First mill in Manchester was forty feet square and two stories high. It had no picker, and the cotton was ginned in the neighborhood at four cents per pound. Spindles only machinery. Mill was shut down from 1816 to 1822, when Olney Robinson of Rhode Island bought it, but was succeeded by Larned Pitcher and Samuel Slater of Pawtucket, R. I. In 1825 they sold three-fifths to Willard Sayles, Lyman Tiffany, Dr. Oliver Dean and Ira Gay. Dean became agent of the company in 1826 and came to Amoskeag.

First Methodist Episcopal Society organized 1829. Built church at Centre, 1830.

First private house built on company's land by Mrs. Anna Heyes of Londonderry, in January, 1839. This house stood on northwest corner of Concord and Chestnut streets, where Tabernacle church now stands.

First white settlers in limits of Manchester were John Goffe, Jr., Edward Lingfield and Benjamin Kidder, who located on Cohas brook near Goffe's Falls in 1722.

First white settlers near Amoskeag Falls were Archibald Stark (father of Gen. Stark), John McNeil, and John Riddell, in 1733.

First yarn spun in mills of Manchester was by Mrs. Stephen Austin, in Stark Mill No. 1, about July, 1839.

Fisk, William H., bookseller, died Aug. 9, 1875, aged 48.

Fling, Daniel W., alderman, assessor, chief engineer, assistant city marshal, died Jan. 11, 1893, aged 82.

Fly-wheel on Amoskeag burst, wrecking boiler house and killing engineer S. J. Bunker and two female operatives and wounding several, Oct. 15, 1891.

Fogg, B. Frank, veteran, and gas fitter, died Sept. 1, 1891, aged 56.

Fogg, Gilman B., veteran gunsmith, died May 30, 1892, aged 71.

HISTORICAL COMPENDIUM — *Continued.*

Fogg, Isaac W., pioneer resident, died Nov. 28, 1891, aged 74.

Fogg, Sewell L., veteran stableman, died May 19, 1892, aged 76.

Foster, Herman, ex-treasurer, died Feb. 17, 1875.

Foresters, Independent Order of:
Uncanoonuc Court, No. 1962, instituted Sept. 2, 1895.

Forest, Knights of Sherwood's Forest:
Conclave Gen. Phil Sheridan, No. 83, organized Nov. 12, 1889.

Forest, Companions of, Queen City Circle, No. 141, organized Dec. 8, 1891.
Maynar Circle, No. 264, organized June, 1893.

Forsaith, Samuel C., business man and manufacturer, died March 23, 1885, aged 57.

Fountain, Currier, placed in front of Amoskeag bank, July 28, 1877.

Fradd, Horatio, ex-state senator, etc., began grocery business 1859.

Free delivery service established by post office, August, 1865.

Freeman, Rev. A. M., resigned from Freewill Baptist church, April 1, 1886.

French, George A., leading insurance man, died Oct. 26, 1886, aged 63.

French, Dr. Leonard, died Feb. 14, 1892, aged 74.

French societies, grand state parade, June 26, 1890.

Freschl, Capt. Joseph, prominent veteran, died Jan. 25, 1890, aged 69.

Foresters of America, Ancient Order of:
Court Granite State, No. 1, instituted April 4, 1881.
Court City of Manchester, No. 3, instituted Nov. 15, 1886.
Court Gen. Stark, No. 7, instituted Sept. 12, 1889.
Court Lafayette, No. 12, instituted Sept. 18, 1891.

Fusileers, Granite, organized Aug. 10, 1842. Samuel W. Parsons first captain. Disbanded about 1860.

HISTORICAL COMPENDIUM — *Continued.*

Gage, Rev. David, Baptist clergyman, died May 10, 1887, aged 86.

Gage, William P., yard overseer of Manchester Mills, died May 9. 1888, aged 59.

Galacar, Jediah, auctioneer, died April 22, 1887, aged 68.

Gamble, John Stark, great grandson of Gen. John Stark, died June 18, 1895, aged 62.

Garland, Rev. F. M., ordained as assistant rector Grace church, April 25, 1893.

Grand Army of the Republic :
    Louis Bell post, No. 3, organized 1868.
    Capt. Joseph Freschl post, No. 94, organized 1890.

Gas Light Co., Manchester, incorporated 1846, re-incorporated July 10, 1850, authorized capital $125,000.   Actual capital 1853, $100,000.   Leased by Peoples Gas Light Co.

Gay, Alpheus, elected mayor by 90 majority, March 9, 1875.

Gibson, Will F., elected principal of Webster-street school, Sept. 3, 1886.

Gillpatrick, Lieut. James, Fourth N. H. V., died in Lawrence, Oct. 26, 1889.

Gleaner, notorious paper, started by John Caldwell, Nov. 12, 1842.

Glidden, Susan, died Sept. 21, aged 92.

Glines, Geo. E., soldier, ex-captain night watch, died May 22, 1895, aged 60.

Goffe, Geo. W., well-known citizen, died July 31, 1895, aged 67.

Good Fellows, Royal Society of, Webster assembly, No. 69, organized April 7, 1887.

Good Templars, Independent Order of :
    Stark lodge, No. 4, organized May 31, 1865.
    Merrimack lodge, No. 5, organized Dec. 6, 1866.
    Harris lodge, No. 45, instituted May 22, 1878.
    Monitor lodge, No. 94 (Swedish), instituted Aug. 31, 1892.

HISTORICAL COMPENDIUM — *Continued.*

Gordon, Rev. L. E., installed over Tabernacle church, April 21, 1878.

Grange, Amoskeag, No. 141, organized August, 1889.

Granite State Trust Co., now Bank of New England, incorporated 1887.

Grocery firm now Allen N. Clapp, began business 1855.

Guards, Clark, organized Jan. 1, 1868. changed name to Haines Rifles, subsequently disbanded.

Guards, Head, organized July 25, 1865. Now Company K, First regiment N. H. N. G.

Guards, National, organized Aug. 17, 1863. Disbanded after the war.

Guards, Sheridan, organized August, 1865.

Guards, Stark, famous military company, organized Aug. 16, 1840. Walter French first captain. Continued about 10 years.

Gymnasium, The. Organized Jan. 4, 1893; incorporated March 23, 1893. Building 168 Amherst street.

Hall, city, built 1845, cost $35,000, repaired 1895 at cost of $18,000.

Hall, G. A. R., Towne's block, dedicated March 5, 1879.

Hall, John B., elected colonel First regiment N. H. N. G., Aug. 4, 1881.

Hall, John B., elected colonel First regiment Aug. 4, 1881.

Hall, Rev. Newton M., ordained July 8, 1891.

Hall, Pythian, Opera block, dedicated May 18, 1881.

Hanover-street church built 1839. Site occupied by north end of Opera House block. It was 80x64 feet in size. Lot given by Amoskeag corporation.

Harrington, E. W., ex-mayor, died at Hot Springs, Ark., July 10, 1876, aged 60.

40

HISTORICAL COMPENDIUM — *Continued.*

Harrison, President Benjamin, visited Manchester Aug. 14, 1893.

Hartshorn, Benj. L., superintendent of streets, died April 2, 1892, aged 52.

Hartmann, Rev. G. F. W., installed at First Presbyterian church, Jan. 27, 1886.

Haskell, Aaron P., original abolitionist, died July 21, 1889, aged 80.

Hatch, Polly, oldest person in Manchester, died April 7, 1883, aged 105.

Hausmann, Rev. H., installed pastor of German Presbyterian church, Jan. 13, 1895.

Hayes, President Rutherford B., visited Manchester, 1887, received by Alderman Devine, acting mayor.

Haynes, Dr. J. O., died April 3, 1881, aged 68.

Heald, Chas. N., of firm of Pike & Heald, died Nov. 19, 1891, aged 64.

Health officers—Geo. B. Swift, Zaccheus Colburn, John D. Kimball, chosen Oct. 26, 1839.

Heath, Albe C., overseer, ex-fireman, etc., died July 17, 1891, aged 72.

Heath, Isaac L., appointed police court judge May 14, 1895.

Heizer, Rev. C. W., installed Jan. 25, 1886, at Unitarian church; resigned

Henrysburg annexed to Derryfield, 1792.

Higgins, Louis, died March 11, 1888, aged 85.

Highest water known in Merrimack, April 15 to 17, 1895.

Hildreth, Joseph W., 31 years in employ of Concord railroad, resigned Jan. 1, 1891.

Hill, Edson, banker and politician, died Jan. 21, 1888, aged 80.

Hill, William H., old time stable-keeper, died March 11, 1895, aged 78.

Hills, Rev. C. D., became pastor of St. Paul's church, April 21, 1891.

HISTORICAL COMPENDIUM — *Continued.*

Historical Society, Manchester, organized Jan. 1, 1896.

History published by Chandler E. Potter, 1856.

Hobbs, Edwin H., Amoskeag superintendent, died Nov. 27. 1890, aged 55.

Hodgman, Charles H., said to be first Union soldier to enter Richmond, died Jan. 10, 1895, aged 57.

Home, Manchester, Children's. Organized Sept. 3, 1884. Building 135 Webster, corner Walnut street, erected 1894, opened April, 1895.

Home, Mercy, East Manchester, dedicated Jan. 1, 1890.

Honor, Knights and Ladies of, Harmony lodge. No. 423, instituted April 20, 1881.

Honor, American Legion of, Rock Rimmon Council, No. 40, instituted Oct. 14, 1879.

Hopkins, George L., elected sub-master High school, Sept. 3, 1880.

Hosley, John, ex-mayor, died March 24, 1890, aged 63.

Hospital, Elliot, completed November, 1889, dedicated April 17, 1890.

Hospital, Elliot, fire at, Mrs. D. Harriman burned to death, May 14, 1890.

Hotel, Amoskeag, burned Jan. 21, 1893.

House for "Merrimack Engine No. 1," first built on Vine street, erected in 1840.

House for agent Stark Mills built by Amoskeag Co., on corner of Hanover and Pine streets. 1839. Also one for Stark superintendent.

Hoyt, Geo. H., who drew first load of dirt from canal where Amory mills now are, died Feb. 6, 1895, aged 85.

Hoyt, John, veteran paper maker, died June 7, 1891, aged 83.

Hoyt, William G., old resident and business man, died Jan. 29, 1893, aged 72.

HISTORICAL COMPENDIUM — *Continued*.

Hubbard, W. F., manufacturer of sash, blinds, etc., succeeds to the business originally established of Hall & Hubbard, in Mechanics Row in 1852.

Hulme, John T., editorial writer on the Union, died June 20, 1887, aged 43.

Huse, Henry H., insurance commissioner, died Sept. 7, 1890, aged 51.

Huse, Isaac, chosen first representative from Manchester, March 12, 1816.

Hutchins, Betsey, completed 50 years employment upon the Stark corporation, May 6, 1895.

Hutchinson, Frank, superintendent of Manchester yard, died Aug. 19, 1893, aged 52.

Hyde, Jared, died Sept. 19, 1894, aged 91.

Institution, Manchester Five Cents Savings, chartered June 26, 1859; name changed to Merrimack River Savings Bank, June 30, 1865.

Insurance Co., N. H. Life, organized Aug. 6, 1886; never did any business.

Insurance Co., Peoples, asked for receiver Sept. 30, 1893.

I. O. O. F., Manchester Unity :
Manchester lodge, No. 7035, instituted 1894.
George Washington lodge, No. 7353, instituted Oct. 15, 1895.

Ireland, Wilberforce, prominent contractor, died April 26, 1892, aged 64.

Iron Hall, Harry E. Webster appointed receiver of, Aug. 26, 1892.

Island Pond House, burned Sept. 18, 1886.

Jackson, Lyman, died Jan. 28, 1887, aged 76.

Jail, county, built in 1863, to accommodate 70 prisoners.

James, Daniel C., stable-keeper, died Nov. 16, 1892, aged 62.

James, George P., 20 years sexton of Universalist church, died May 16, 1894 aged 71.

James, Jacob F., ex mayor, died April 15, 1892, aged —.

43

HISTORICAL COMPENDIUM -- *Continued.*

Jencks, Welcome, inventor, died Dec. 12, 1891, aged 70.

Jewell, Joseph, old resident, died Nov. 23, 1887, aged 80.

Johnson, Edward P., coal merchant, died May 28, 1892, aged 72.

Johnson, Jeremiah, member of the Manchester Rifles, killed at muster in Goffs-town by Elbridge Ford in an affray with gamblers. Ford served three years in prison for the crime.

Johnson, Rev. N. G., resigned from Swedish Presbyterian church March 30, 1894.

Jones, Jeremiah D., prominent musician, died July 18. 1893, aged 66.

Karver, Rev. Geo. N., installed pastor of Westminster Presbyterian church Dec. 14, 1887.

Kelly, John L., ex-mayor, died May 1, 1887, aged 76. Had been fire engineer, tax collector, city marshal, etc., and was a veteran soldier.

Kennard, Dimond, real estate owner, died April 14, 1891, aged 74.

Kennard, James, large real estate owner, died Sept. 7, 1886.

Kennard, Joseph F., ex-alderman, state senator, died Nov. 7, 1892, aged 67.

Kidder, Maria F., elected assistant in high school Jan. 2, 1875.

Kidder, Samuel B., old resident, died Dec. 4, 1885, aged 79.

Killey, William L., ex-agent Stark mills, died May 27, 1893, aged 76.

Kimball Bros., leased Manchester shoe factory Aug. 31, 1886.

Kimball, Rev. Clarion H., installed at First Baptist church ; resigned 1888.

Kimball, Ezra, a well-known citizen, died Jan. 21, 1875.

Kimball, C. Howard, well-known newspaper man, died Aug. 6, 1893, aged 42.

44

HISTORICAL COMPENDIUM — *Continued.*

Kimball, Prof. Jason J., 22 years teacher of music in public schools, died Sept. 27, 1895, aged 66.

Kimball, Matthew G., killed by falling down stairs, April 15, 1892, aged 87.

King, A. F., elected principal of Ash-street school, Aug. 4, 1893; resigned 1895.

Knight, Albert F., succeeded William E. Winsor as agent of Amory mills, April 14, 1891: resigned Jan. 1, 1896.

Knights of Honor:
Temple lodge, No. 2065, instituted Feb. 27, 1880.
Alpine lodge, No. 2886, instituted Dec. 28, 1882.

Knights of Pythias:
Granite lodge, No. 3, instituted April 8, 1870.
Merrimack lodge, No. 4, instituted May 6, 1870.
Queen City lodge, No. 35, instituted Dec. 10, 1889.
Rock Rimmon lodge, No. 44, instituted July 8, 1892.
Golden Rule lodge, No. 45, instituted Sept. 14, 1892.

Knowlton, Ebenezer G., resident since 1840, died March 22, 1888, aged 91.

Knowlton, Edgar J., elected mayor Nov. 5, 1890, by 119 plurality over Thos. W. Lane; Tuttle, R., had 594 plurality for governor; Taggart, R., 156 for congress; Ramsdell, R., 590 for councillor.

Knowlton, Edgar J., nominated as postmaster April 13, 1894; received commission May 5; resigned as mayor May 10.

Laboratory, Manchester print works, burned June 12, 1888; loss $40,000.

Land sale, fourth, by the Amoskeag Co., Sept. 30, 1845. Land bounded by Elm, Lowell, Union, and Orange streets sold.

Lane, G. M. L., elected colonel First regiment Dec. 3, commissioned Dec. 21, 1886.

Lane, Warren L., appointed postmaster 1845.

Leach, David R., died April 2, 1878, aged 71.

45

FOR PROTECTION

HISTORICAL COMPENDIUM — *Continued.*

League, Citizens', formed April 24, 1888. Many liquor dealers raided that week.

Leavell, Rev. W. H., installed pastor First Baptist church, May 7, 1877.

Librarians, City, Francis B. Eaton. 1854; Marshall P. Hall, 1863; Ben: F. Stanton, 1865; Charles H. Marshall, 1866; Mrs. M. J. Buncher, —; Miss Kate E. Sanborn, 1895.

Library, Social, of Derryfield, organized 1795; dissolved 1833. Manchester Athenaeum organized Feb. 19, 1844; transferred its property to the city in 1854, and public free library was founded with 3000 books. Nearly destroyed by fire in Patten's block, Feb. 5, 1856. Removed to city library building, which cost $30,000, July, 1871.

Library, free, established 1854; building erected 1871.

Lighting, electric, introduced Aug. 23, 1882.

Lincoln, Abraham, spoke in Manchester 1860, in Smyth's hall. Introduced by Frederick Smyth.

Lincoln club, Manchester, organized March 7, 1888.

Livermore, Col. Thos. L., appointed agent of Amoskeag corporation March 24, 1879.

Lockhart, Rev. Burton W., installed at Franklin-street church, Jan. 24, 1894.

Locomotive Works, started as Vulcan Works 1853, chartered 1854.

Lord, John, died April 28, 1883, aged 86.

Lord, Samuel D., attorney, former city solicitor, legislator, etc., died Feb. 23, 1850, aged 63.

—

HISTORICAL COMPENDIUM — *Continued.*

Lot, Gen. Stark engine house, bought September, 1886; cost $1,286.50.

Lowell-street Universalist church, B. M. Tillotson, pastor, dedicated February, 1840; cost $6,500.

Loyal Orange Institution :
Mt. Sinai lodge, No. 38, instituted Dec. 8, 1880.
George Washington Temperance lodge, No. 296, instituted Nov. 5, 1894.

Loyal Orange Ladies' Institution :
Derryfield Purple Star lodge, No. 71, chartered July 7, 1894.

Lyceum, Manchester, organized 1842.

Maben, Rev. B. S., installed pastor of Christian church Nov. 30, 1892; resigned Nov. 18, 1893.

Machine shop, old Amoskeag, built 1840. Second or new shop built 1848. Locomotives were made in 1849, and in 1859 steam fire engines. The first continued but a few years when it was sold to the Locomotive works, which afterward acquired the fire-engine business.

Mack, Dea. Daniel K., oldest native born resident of West Manchester, ex-representative, etc., died Feb. 9, 1895, aged 73.

Mack, Dea. Benj., died Aug. 13, 1878, aged 89.

Malvern, Rev. Lewis, pastor of Merrimack-street Baptist church March 8, 1880, to December, 1882.

Manahan, Lucretia E., respected teacher for 36 years, died Jan. 29, 1892, aged 56.

Manchester House, old, sold at auction Dec. 21, 1887, for $74,100. It was built in 1839. The site and what is now Merrimack square were then covered with pitch pines.

Manchester made separate representative district, 1815.

Manchester, so named in 1810 in compliment to Judge Blodgett, who said it should become "the Manchester of America."

47

HISTORICAL COMPENDIUM — *Continued.*

Marden, William G., then oldest stone cutter in city, died May 1, 1892, aged —.

Marshall, Dustin, old resident, died Jan. 14, 1892, aged 74.

Martin, Col. Benj. F., paper-maker, died June 16, 1886.

Massabesic, first electric car ran over road to, Aug. 5, 1895.

Mason, Jeremiah B., old resident, died Sept. 14, 1894, aged 83.

Masonry:
Lafayette lodge moved from Bedford to Manchester, 1845.
Mount Horeb Royal Arch chapter chartered September, 1847.
Trinity commandery, K. T., moved to Manchester from Lebanon.
Adoniram council, R. & S. M., chartered September, 1856.
Washington lodge began work under dispensation, January, 1857.
May, 1863, Winslow Lewis Lodge of Perfection organized; consolidated shortly with Aaron P. Hughes lodge of Nashua.

Mayors—First, Hiram Brown, 1846-47, elected after two attempts; second, Jacob F. James, 1847-48, elected at fourth trial, served two terms; third, Warren L. Lane, elected Oct. 3, 1849, on fifth trial; fourth, Moses Fellows, served 1850-1852; fifth, 1852-1855, Frederick Smyth; sixth, Theodore T. Abbot, 1855-1857; seventh, Jacob F. James, 1857-1858; eighth, Alonzo Smith, 1858; ninth, E. W. Harrington, 1859 and 1860; tenth, David A. Bunton, 1861 and 1862; eleventh, Theodore T. Abbot, 1863; twelfth, Frederick Smyth, 1864; thirteenth, Darwin J. Daniels, 1865, died May 31; fourteenth, John Hosley, elected to fill vacancy; re-elected 1866; fifteenth, Joseph B. Clark, 1866; sixteenth, James A. Weston, 1867; seventeenth, Isaac W. Smith, 1868; eighteenth, James A. Weston, 1870 and 1871; nineteenth, Person C. Cheney, 1872; twentieth, Charles H. Bartlett, 1873, resigned Feb. 18; twenty-first, John P. Newell, elected to fill vacancy, 1873; twenty-second, James A. Weston, 1874; twenty-third, Alpheus Gay, 1875; twenty-fourth, Ira Cross, 1876, 1877, resigned; twenty-fifth, John L. Kelly, elected to fill vacancy Sept. 4, 1877, re-elected and served till January, 1881; twenty-sixth, Horace B. Putnam, served four

48

HISTORICAL COMPENDIUM — *Continued.*

years; twenty-seventh, George H. Stearns, 1885-1886; twenty-eighth. John Hosley, 1887-1888; twenty-ninth, David B. Varney, 1889-1890; thirtieth, Edgar J. Knowlton, 1891-1894, resigned; thirty-first, Byron Worthen, acting mayor to fill out term; thirty-second, Wm. C. Clarke, 1895—. Mayoralty elections were annual till 1878; biennial since; by majority till act of legislature in 1849, when it was changed to plurality.

Maynard, "Uncle" John H., 50 years a resident, died May 5, 1894, aged 90.

McAllister, Police Sergt. Henry, murdered May 22, 1895, by ex-policeman Fred A. Stockwell. The latter was sentenced to 30 years in state prison in December.

McCrillis, John B., carriage maker, died Nov. 27, 1885, aged 70.

McDonald, Rev. William, pioneer Catholic priest, died Aug. 26, 1885, aged 72.

McDuffie, Charles D., elected agent Manchester mills Sept. 22, 1880; began duties Oct. 1.

McGregor, James, a pioneer citizen, died July 7, 1893, aged 73.

McKean, Leonard, died Sept. 4, 1882, aged 68.

McKinney, Rev. L. F., became pastor of Lowell-street Universalist church May 1, 1875; retired June 28, 1885. He was appointed minister to Colombia, April 25, 1893.

McLellan, Rev. Bryant, resigned from Advent pastorate 1885.

McQueston, Lucinda F., veteran school teacher, died June 15, 1891.

Mechanics, Order United American, Granite State Council, No. 1, organized March 24, 1873. Disbanded about 1878.

"Mechanics Row," famous for small manufactories; abolished in 1886 when the Jefferson mill was built.

Meeting-house, first built in town, erected in 1736, soon after destroyed in a woods fire.

Meeting-house converted into town-house, 1836, at cost of $500.

HISTORICAL COMPENDIUM — *Continued.*

Memorial, second newspaper, started Jan. 1, 1840, by Joseph C. Emerson. Name changed subsequently to Manchester American.

"Merchants' Exchange," cost $72,000 to build. Its annual rent-roll is $25,000 or more.

Merrimack square, northeast corner of, accepted Feb. 1, 1841, by vote of 162 to 91.

Merrimack, Engine, No. 1, first fire engine owned by town, purchased 1839. (Piscataquog, then part of Bedford, had a fire engine in 1818.)

Mill, "Bell," and mill "Old," burned March 28, 1848. These mills occupied the site of the P. C. Cheney Paper Co.'s mills.

Mill, "Island," burned May 14, 1840.

Mills, Amoskeag, Nos. 1 and 2 built in 1841; No. 3 in 1844, rebuilt 1870; No. 4, 1846, enlarged 1872; No. 5 built 1855; No. 6, 1859-60; No. 7, 1874; No. 8, 1875; No. 9, 1880; No. 10 (Jefferson mill), 1886; No. 11, 1889.

Mills, Amory, built 1880, started up Aug. 10.

Mills at Goffe's Falls were first built about 1749 by Col. John Goffe.

Mills, Derry, organized 1865; capital $100,000; now known as Devonshire mills.

Mills, Devonshire, incorporated 1886.

Mills, Langdon, incorporated 1846, 1853 and 1857, but not organized till 1860. No. 1 mill was built by the Blodget Paper Co. after 1853. No. 2 mill was built 1868.

Mills, Manchester, incorporated 1839. First mill built 1845. Second mill built 1850. Printery burned 1852. Half of largest mill burned July 13, 1855; loss $271,353. George B. Upton was first agent, succeeded by William P. Newell in 1845, and Watemo Smith taking charge of mills in 1848.

HISTORICAL COMPENDIUM — *Continued.*

Mills, Manchester, incorporated 1839, first mill built in 1847; name changed to Manchester Print Works 1849; capital increased to $1,800,000 in 1852; during the war declared five successive semi-annual dividends of 10 per cent. each ; capital reduced to $540,000, and concern sold at auction 1874; bought by the Manchester Print Works and mills with a capital of $2,000,-000.

Mills, Manchester, No. 1 built 1844, partially burned 1855 and rebuilt; No. 2 built 1850; No. 3 completed 1879. No. 4 canal building built about 1862; No. 5 built 1884-1887; No. 6 built 1871.

Mills, saw and grist, were built by Col. Moses Kelley of Goffstown at Kelley's Falls soon after the Revolution.

Mills, Namaske, organized as Amoskeag Duck and Bag mills, 1856; changed to Namaske mills, 1869; mill built in 1856 and sold to Amoskeag Co. Feb. 26, 1875 ; now occupied by A. P. Olzendam as a hosiery mill.

Mills, saw and grist, were built near outlet of Lake Massabesic as early as 1742 by John McMurphy.   Site now called " Webster's Mills."

Mills, saw and grist, were built on the Piscataquog river where the James Baldwin Co. is now located, as early as 1779 by Samuel Moor.

Mills, Stark, chartered 1838: officers elected Sept. 26, 1838.   No. 1 mill built 1838; No. 2, in 1839; No. 3, in 1846.   West Side mill built in 1889.

Mission, McAuley Rescue, organized Feb. 23, 1892, opened March 26, 1892. Rooms, 36 Merrimack St.

Mitchell, James, old resident, died Nov. 26, 1880, aged 92.

Monument, Soldiers', dedicated Sept. 11, 1879: cost about $22,000.

Moody and Sankey revival meetings, November, 1877.

Moore, Capt. Ira A., hotel-keeper and Amoskeag Veteran, died Dec. 13, 1887, aged 54.

Moore, J. Bailey, old time newspaper man, died May 11, 1893, aged 78.

51

HISTORICAL COMPENDIUM -- *Continued.*

Moore, Hon. John P., held many public offices, died Sept. 13, 1888, aged 67.

Moore, John W., musical critic and composer, died March 23, 1889, aged 81.

Morrill, Charles F., bank cashier, disappeared July 26, 1893.

Morrill, Nathaniel E., pioneer citizen and Odd Fellow, died March 8, 1890, aged 77.

Morrison, George W., lawyer and ex-congressman, died Dec. 21, 1888, aged 79. Opened law office in Manchester in 1836. Opposed Kansas-Nebraska acts, and lost caste as a Democrat.

Morrison, Rev. William H., installed pastor Lowell-street Universalist church, Nov. 1, 1885.

Moulton, Emerson, old resident, 28 years reed manufacturer, died Sept. 28, 1893, aged 66.

Moulton, Henry B., overseer Amoskeag yard, died Jan. 14, 1882, aged 59.

Mowatt, Dea. H. T., died Jan. 10, 1878, aged 72.

Murkland, Rev. Charles S., installed at Franklin-street church, April 6, 1886, resigned June 11, 1893; accepted presidency agricultural college July 1.

Murphy, Michael, who carried first dispatch announcing attack on Fort Sumter, died Jan. 14, 1890.

Muskets, 40,000, made for government by Amoskeag Co. during the war.

Nay, A. J., noted book canvasser, died June 24, 1891.

New England Order of Protection :
    Star lodge, No. 23, chartered Dec. 31, 1887.

Newell, William P., died Aug. 11, 1885, aged 78.

Nichols, John C., veteran stable-keeper, died Sept. 17, 1892, aged 73.

Nichols, Joseph, real estate owner and old resident, died Oct. 28, 1894, aged 74.

HISTORICAL COMPENDIUM -- *Continued.*

Norris. Rev. G. W., installed over St. Paul's M. E. church, April 21, 1878.

Nutt, Major Rodma, died Jan. 23, 1875. He was the first child born after the city was incorporated, and was the father of the celebrated dwarf, Commodore Nutt.

Oakes, Rev. E. W., resigned from Tabernacle Baptist church, Nov. '13, 1891

Odd Fellowship:
Hillsborough lodge, No. 2, instituted Dec. 21, 1843.
Wonolancet encampment, No. 2, instituted Sept. 6, 1844.
Mechanics lodge, No. 13, instituted Nov. 25, 1845.
Wildey lodge, No. 45, instituted Aug. 8, 1866.
Mt. Washington encampment, No. 16, instituted March 2, 1871.
Ridgely lodge, No. 74, instituted Feb. 17, 1887, with 133 members.
Uncanoonuc lodge, No. 86, instituted March, 1893.
Social Rebekah Degree lodge, No. 10, instituted April 26, 1875.
Arbutus Rebekah Degree lodge, No. 51, instituted May 17, 1893.
Mistletoe Rebekah Degree lodge, No. 57, instituted Jan. 11, 1894.
Block, Odd Fellows, built 1872, dedicated April 26.

O'Mally, P. H., elected captain of Head Guards, succeeding John H. Wales, Jr., Dec. 13, 1886.

Opera house, Manchester, opened Jan. 24, 1881.

O. U. A. M.:
Ben Franklin council, No. 1, instituted July 8, 1850.
Gen. Stark council, No. 6, instituted Sept. 7, 1888.
Evening Star council, No. 10, instituted Aug. 7, 1891.
Sunset council, No. 16, instituted Jan. 26, 1893.

Palmer & Garmon, marble workers, succeed to the business established by C. H. Winslow in 1842, J. B. Campbell following in 1846, Chase & Palmer in 1855, Palmer & Farnham in 1856, J. D. Palmer in 1867, Palmer & Garmon in 1871. Lamson & Marden started in 1849, and Palmer & Garmon succeeded to their business also in 1871.

Pan-American Congress representatives visited the mills, Oct. 8, 1889.

HISTORICAL COMPENDIUM — *Continued.*

Paper mills, Amoskeag, incorporated 1887.

Park, Rev. George M., installed over Merrimack-street F. W. Baptist church, November, 1874; resigned Dec. 3, 1879.

Park, Stark, dedicated June 17, 1893.

Parker, Gustavus D., seaman, soldier, shoemaker, died Jan. 17, 1894, aged 61.

Parker, Jonas L., tax collector, murdered March 26, 1845. Perpetrator never convicted.

Parker, John O., ex-councilman, etc., died Feb. 17, 1890, aged 65.

Parker, Nathan, ex-councillor, banker, died May 6, 1894, aged 86.

Parsons, Capt. Samuel W., prominent in early military circles, builder and real estate owner, died July 31, 1886.

Patten, Alfred F., 44 years freight master Concord railroad, died Feb. 23, 1893, aged 66.

Payne, Rev. E. B., resigned from Unitarian church, Oct. 1, 1885.

Peabody, Deacon Joseph, died Feb. 24, 1890, aged 74.

Pearson, Dr. Edwin O., died Oct. 28, 1886.

Pearson, Moses O., prominent veteran and fraternity man, died Oct. 9, 1886.

Perkins, David P., is sole survivor of the original members of the Second Baptist church, and was first male instructor in the old high school building on Lowell St., opened June, 1841.

Perkins, Nathaniel, resident for 55 years, died May 19, 1894, aged 74.

Perry, William G., former superintendent on the Amoskeag, died in Hampton Nov. 9, 1887, aged 70.

Peter, Rev. Brother, formerly principal of parochial high school, died in New York Jan. 13, 1894.

Pettee, Holmes R., grain dealer, died Feb. 22, 1892, aged 70.

HISTORICAL COMPENDIUM — *Continued.*

Pettigrew, James W., old time hair merchant, Mexican war veteran, died Jan. 1, 1892, aged 69.

Pickering, J. Edward, elected master of North Main-street school, Oct. 18, 1886.

Pierce, Col. Thomas P., appointed postmaster 1853.

Pierce, Capt. Nathan H., veteran of 8th N. H. V., died Nov. 26, 1887, aged 62.

Pike, Rufus H., 45 years in stove business, died Jan. 8, 1895, aged 65.

Pilgrim Fathers, J. E. Shepherd colony, organized Dec. 13, 1888.

Pillsbury, Huldah W., oldest weaver in the city, died Jan. 24, 1890, aged 80.

Piper, Lieut. John K., merchant and veteran, died April 1, 1890, aged 56.

Piper, S. S., received commission as postmaster, May 5, 1890.

Piscataquog and Amoskeag, parts of Bedford and Goffstown respectively, annexed to Manchester, 1853.

Plurality elected mayor, 1849, elected other city and ward officers, 1856.

Police court, Judges of, Samuel D. Bell, assumed office 1846; Chandler E. Potter, 1848; Isaac W. Smith, 1855; Samuel Upton, 1857; Joseph W. Fellows, 1874; Nathan P. Hunt, 1876; Isaac L. Heath, 1895.

Police officers — Hiram Brown, Nehemiah Chase, J. T. P. Hunt, and James Wallace appointed first police officers, Nov. 28, 1839.

Police system, as of town of Portsmouth, adopted Oct. 26, 1839.

Population 1830, 887.
1840, 3,325.
1850, 13,932.
1860, 20,107.
1870, 23,536.
1880, 32,630.
1890, 42,983.
1895, not less than 55,000.

HISTORICAL COMPENDIUM — *Continued.*

Porter, Charles C. P., Amoskeag overseer, died April 7, 1884, aged 69.

Post, Louis Bell, G. A. R., organized Jan. 20, 1868; incorporated March 3, 1869; adopted name Dec. 9, 1869.

Post-office : At Centre, established 1831, with Albert Jackson as postmaster; in 1840 an office was established in Duncklee's block and Jesse Duncklee was made postmaster; Duncklee died in March and was succeeded by Paul Cragin, Jr.; when town hall was built in 1841 it was moved to it; in 1844, when the city hall was burned, it was moved to Cragin's house on Hanover St., subsequently to a 10-footer on Hanover St.; and when the new city hall was built, it occupied the southwest corner. Subsequent postmasters were Warren L. Lane, 1845; James Hersey, 1849; Thomas F. Pierce, 1853; David J. Clark, 1861; Bradbury P. Cilley, 1865; Joseph L. Stevens, 1870; Josiah G. Dearborn, 1886; Samuel S. Piper, 1890; Edgar J. Knowlton, 1894. In 1854 the office was moved to corner of Hanover St., where Fitt's Little 5 now is.

Pound voted to be built 1800, located at south end of meeting-house lot at Centre, and used till 1830.

Pratt, Alvin, old time baker, died Jan. 5, 1891, aged 72.

Print-works, Manchester, first printery built 1845, burned in 1853, and rebuilt.

Putnam, Horace B., elected mayor Nov. 3, 1880, by 728 plurality; re-elected 1882; died April 20, 1888, aged 62.

Putnam, Sylvanus B., city treasurer 16 years, died Nov. 11, 1895, aged 60.

Putney, Philip B., veteran Odd Fellow and caterer, charter member Amoskeag Veterans, died Sept. 15, 1888, aged 77.

Quimby, Mrs. Mehitable, 60 years a resident and a worker in first mill at Amoskeag, died Nov. 12, 1889, aged 78.

Quint, Col. A. W., politician and business man, committed suicide by hanging while temporarily insane, Oct. 7, 1887, aged 61.

HISTORICAL COMPENDIUM — *Continued.*

Quint, Isaac, 40 years employed on Amoskeag, died Aug. 17, 1886, aged 63.

Railroad, Concord, opened through town June 28, 1842. Public opening July 4, when thousands rode free to Nashua.

Railroad, Concord & Montreal, leased to Boston & Maine June 29, 1895.

Railroad, Manchester & Lawrence, opened to Manchester Nov. 13, 1849.

Ramsay, Rev. William H., installed pastor of Unitarian church, June 3, 1892. resigned from church, March 21, 1894.

Rand, Jonathan, first school-master whose name has been preserved.

Rankin, Major Abel C., gallant soldier, died Oct. 21, 1889, aged 57.

Red Men, Improved Order :
Passaconnaway tribe, No. 5, instituted April 12, 1881.
Agawam tribe, No. 8, instituted Sept. 15, 1886, with 180 charter members.

Reed, Capt. C. H., soldier and policeman, died Sept. 23, 1892, aged 50.

Report, town, first voted to be printed March 15, 1843. Annual reports began to be published 1842.

Representative, first newspaper in Manchester, established Oct. 18, 1839, by John Caldwell. Sold in December, 1842, to Kimball & Kidder, publishers of the Manchester Democrat.

Reservoir, Manchester Centre, has capacity of 16,000,000 gallons, and is 152 feet above Elm street, and 188 feet above Canal street at passenger station.

Reynolds, Henry C., agent Amoskeag Axe Co., died Jan. 12, 1877.

Rhodes, Rev. Harry J., left Christian church to become missionary to Japan, August, 1889.

Rice, Joseph B., 18 years Manchester mills overseer, died Jan. 26, 1889, aged 77.

HISTORICAL COMPENDIUM — *Continued.*

Ricker, Jedediah C., captain of Granite Fusileers, 27 years in Amoskeag machine shop, foreman Amoskeag Fire Co., No. 1, etc., died April 19, 1888, aged 69.

Riddle, Col. George W., prominent business man, connected with agricultural fairs, etc., died Jan. 18, 1893, aged 67.

Riddle, Gilman, pioneer citizen, died May 15, 1893, aged 81.

Riddle, Isaac, old resident and business man, died Oct. 3, 1875, aged 82.

Ridlon, Rev. G. T., resigned from Christian church, 1885.

Rifles, Smyth, organized August, 1865; disbanded a few years later.

Rifles, Straw, organized March 17, 1873; subsequently named City Guards, and Scammon Rifles; disbanded November, 1895.

Risvold, Ingvold, 25 years at Locomotive works, died Sept. 20, 1888.

Road, Mammoth, designed for a direct line from Concord to Lowell, first suggested in February, 1823. Finally ordered to be built by court in 1830, but not built till 1834.

Road, Nutt, laid out Sept. 22, 1840.

Roberts, Stephen H., dyer, soldier, and K. P., died March 17, 1888, aged 58.

Robinson, Nathan T., Amoskeag card room overseer, shot himself Dec. 26, 1889, aged 49.

Rock Rimmon is 116½ feet from lowest to highest point of rock. Its top is 188 feet above the city hall steps, and 260 feet above the Merrimack.

Rowell, Joseph M., old resident, died Dec. 19, 1894, aged 88.

Runnels, Samuel H., color-bearer Fourth N. H. V., fell at Universalist church July 9, 1878, died 10th.

Russia, contributions amounting to $1,507.08 sent from Manchester, April 4, 1892.

HISTORICAL COMPENDIUM — *Continued.*

Ryder, Charles G. B., real estate dealer, died July 22, 1882, aged 56.

Sanborn, Gustavus M., insurance man for 20 years, died June 10, 1889, aged 73.

Sanborn, Miss Kate E., elected city librarian Feb. 5, 1894.

Savings Bank, Guaranty, incorporated 1879.

Sawin, Rev. T. Parsons, died Jan. 19, 1886, aged 68.

School, "Ecole des Sts. Anges," opened Dec. 13, 1885.

School, evening, first held 1854, then omitted till 1868, and has since been continued.

School, first high, corner of Lowell and Chestnut streets, built 1841. Lot given by Amoskeag Co.; building cost $3,000.

School, high, established 1848, John W. Ray master, salary $800.

School, Park street grammar, established as a parochial school 1861, adopted as public school 1863, with Thomas Corcoran principal, discontinued as such till 1869; continued as parochial school till lot was bought by Catholics and sold for business purposes 1894.

School, parochial, first opened in basement of St. Ann's church, January, 1859. Thomas Corcoran, teacher.

School, Rimmon, formally opened Sept. 10, 1894.

School, State Industrial, commissioners appointed 1855; bought the Gen. Stark farm for $10,000, and 10 acres additional for $1,000. Building was erected in 1856 and 1857, and furnished in 1858, costing $34,000. Dedicated May 12, 1858. Brooks Shattuck was first superintendent, serving to April 20, 1866, when he was succeeded by Isaac H. Jones. Jones served till May 17, 1870. John C. Ray succeeded him July 2, 1874, and has served to date.

School-districts changed in 1809, and school-house built at the Centre.

School-house, Ash-street, built 1874, cost $60,000.

HISTORICAL COMPENDIUM — *Continued.*

School-house, first in Derryfield, built in 1795, on Falls road in rear of residence of Hon. David Cross, by private subscription. Town voted to buy
this house and build two others in 1798.

School-house, Lincoln-street, built 1874, cost $50,000.

School-house, new high, plans for, adopted May 22, 1895; cost $100,000.

School-house, old Falls, burned 1859.

School-house, old high, first built for a district school; David P. Perkins was
the first master, salary $267.

School-house, Straw, occupied Sept. 23, 1895.

School-house, Varney, dedicated Dec. 26, 1890.

School-houses: Old high, built ——: Park-street, built 1847; Webster's
mills, about 1847; Spring-street, 1848; house corner Merrimack and
Union, 1856; Franklin-street, 1857; Blodgett-street, 1859; Massabesic,
1860; Mosquito Pond, 1860; Amoskeag, 1860; Harvey's mills, 1865;
High, 1863, now being rebuilt; Main-street, 1870; Goffe's Falls, 1870;
Stark district, 1871; Lincoln-street, 1871; Ash-street, 1874.

Schools, Roman Catholic parochial, established in 1861 and before. In 1863
adopted by the city. Teachers were nominated by Rev. Wm. MacDonald,
and wore the garb of the Sisters of Mercy. In 1868 the city discontinued
its support of them, and since they have been supported entirely at the
charge of the Catholics.

Schools, superintendent of, elected 1854.
  "   "   1855–1859, James O. Adams.
  "   "   1859–1860, John W. Ray.
  "   "   1860–1867, James O. Adams.
  "   "   1867–1875, Joseph E. Edgerly.
  "   "   1875–1877, Josiah G. Dearborn.
  "   "   1877–   William E. Buck.

Scott, William P., aged war veteran, died Dec. 23, 1893, aged 72.

CAVANAUGH BROS.,

• • • •

Headquarters for Horses in New Hampshire.

● ● ● ●

WEST CENTRAL STREET.

HISTORICAL COMPENDIUM — *Continued.*

Scottish Clans, Order of, Clan McKenzie, No. 27, organized April 7, 1887.

Sears, Rev. Lorenzo, resigned from Grace church rectorship Nov. 1, 1885.

Second land sale, Oct. 8, 1839. Lots between Hanover and Merrimack, Elm and Union streets, sold. Prices much higher than at previous sale.

Selden, Rev. Edward G., ordained and installed pastor of First Congregational church, Dec. 16, 1873; resigned May 3, 1885.

Semi-Centennial celebration, probably Sept. 8, 1896.

Senter, Charles J., clothing merchant for 20 years, died Dec. 29, 1887, aged 40.

Severance, William, of Severance beach, Massabesic, died March 6, 1891, aged 70.

Shattuck, Fred W., resigned as principal Lincoln grammar school, Oct. 7, 1886.

Shea, Capt. D. F., resigned from Sheridan Guards, May 13, 1894, succeeded by William Sullivan.

Shea, Daniel, first victim of contempt clause of nuisance act, jailed May 18, 1888.

Shirley, Robert M., old resident, died Jan. 20, 1889, aged 81.

Shoe factory, Manchester, opened Nov. 14, 1885.

Shop, Hodge's, explosion of boiler at, May 8, 1888, W. H. H. Tyler and H. D. Atwood killed.

Signs removed from over sidewalks, July 1, 1891.

Simons, Hiram, died June 1, 1882, aged 77.

Simons, Major Lewis, Amoskeag Veteran and real estate owner, died Oct. 6, 1895, aged 80.

Small-pox epidemic, 1792.

Smith, Mary A., principal of Webster school, resigned Aug. 1, 1886.

Smith, Waterman, former agent of Manchester mills, died Aug. 5, 1892, aged 76.

Smyth, Mrs. Frederick, died Jan. 14, 1885, aged 63.

HISTORICAL COMPENDIUM — *Continued.*

Society, First Congregational, formed at Amoskeag April 4, 1838; in 1839 built first church on Hanover street, for which the Amoskeag Co. gave the land, and the Stark mills $500. In 1846 changed name to First Congregational Society in Manchester.

Society, German School. Organized 1879. Meets in school-house corner Ferry and Third streets, last Tuesday in each month.

Society, Manchester City Missionary, legally organized April 24, 1850, though its work had been going on since 1847. Building erected in 1850 on land given by Amoskeag Co.

Society, Manchester Ladies' Aid and Relief, organized January, 1875. Hospital, 180 Pearl; building and lot gift of Aretas Blood.

Society, Manchester Washington Total Abstinence, organized Aug. 3, 1841; at one time had 2000 members.

Society, St. Augustine. Organized June 20, 1878.

Society, Second Methodist, built chapel on Hanover street, 1840.

Society, St. Jean Baptiste. Organized April 13, 1871. Meets first and third Fridays in G. A. R. hall.

Sons of St. George, Hearts of Oak Lodge, No. 91, instituted April 6, 1882.

Spalding, Rev. George E., installed over Franklin-street church Feb. 14, 1883; resigned Sept. 6, 1885.

Speed, Benjamin, 30 years Amoskeag overseer, died Sept. 3, 1886, aged 75.

Spencer, John S., 21 years Stark overseer, died July 24, 1890, aged 61.

Sperry, Rev. Wm. G., installed at Hanover-street Congregational church Oct. 6, 1885; resigned Nov. 27, 1892.

Spofford, John T., assistant postmaster 32 years, retired May 5, 1894.

Squares, Concord, Merrimack and Tremont, deeded to the city 1848; Hanover in 1852.

Staples, Rev. Charles L., began pastorate at Unitarian church, Jan. 13, 1895.

Star, Order of Eastern, Ruth chapter, organized 1893.

Stark, Major Caleb, eldest son of Gen. Stark, born Dec. 23, 1759, died Aug. 26, 1838, in Ohio. He was at Bunker Hill though but 16 years old, and served throughout the Revolution, being adjutant-general of the northern department in 1781.

Stark, John, Esq., called " Justice Stark," after the people of the " new village " had won at the town meeting of 1840, advanced to the moderator's desk and made this speech: " Who are ye that are here to act and tread upon us in this manner? I'll tell ye who you are — you 're a set of interlopers come here to get a living upon a sand bank, and a d—d poor living you will get, let me tell ye ! "

Stark, Gen. John, died May 8, 1822. Born in Londonderry, Aug. 28, 1728. Famous for battle at Bennington, and service in colonial and Revolutionary war. Buried in family ground in what is now Stark park.

State divided into five counties, Derryfield attached to Hillsborough, so named from Willis Hills, Earl of Hillsborough, member of George III.'s privy council. 1771.

Station, passenger, built 1855.

Steamer Fire King won first prize at Lawrence muster, playing 218 feet 2½ inches, Oct. 13, 1886.

Stearns, Hiram, policeman for many years and janitor at Franklin-street church, died Dec. 7, 1894, aged 74.

Stearns, Hiram, ex-councilman, 40 years employed by Amoskeag mills, died Aug. 9, 1895, aged 77.

Stevens, Benjamin, built a saw mill on Amoskeag brook, now called Cemetery brook, and which flowed into the Merrimack at that time a few rods north of Granite bridge, about 1736. Its sills were found when the foundations were dug for the Manchester print works.

Stevens, Daniel L., deputy sheriff for 36 years, old resident, died July 24, 1893, aged 76.

Stevens, Mrs. Hannah, mother of 16 children, died Sept. 14, 1894, aged 79.

Stevens, Horace E., 31 years in grocery business, died Dec. 25, 1886, aged 50.

Stevens, Joseph L., appointed postmaster, 1870.

Stickney, Jeremiah, veteran dealer in rubber goods, died Dec. 9, 1892.

Stoekle, Rev. Frederick C., of German Presbyterian church, died Aug. 2, 1894. aged 33.

Stokes, Moses D., died July 17, 1882, aged 76.

Stokes, Orrin B., claimed to be the champion drummer of the world, died April 15, 1895, aged 48.

Stone, Joseph, resigned as agent Manchester mills, Oct. 1, 1880.

Story, Dr. Abram B., died Feb. 23, 1893. aged 72.

Strain, Capt. C. W., veteran of 10th N. H. V., died Feb. 4, 1891.

Straw, Ezekiel A., ex-Governor, agent Amoskeag mills, died Oct. 23, 1882, aged 63.

Straw, James B., elected auditor Jan. 7, 1890, died Jan. 21, 1894, aged 62.

Street, Park, renamed Lake avenue, Sept. 7, 1886.

Strike, great, March 20, 1855, against change in working hours, lasted eight days. Unsuccessful strike, Amoskeag, began Feb. 15, 1886, lasted till March 5.

Sturgis, Dr. James G., veteran and leading physician, died Oct. 16, 1889, aged 52.

Sullivan, Henry C., 40 years employee of the Amoskeag, died March 21, 1887, aged 81.

Sutcliffe, Frank S., transferred from North Main-street to Lincoln grammar school, Oct. 18, 1886. F. W. Shattuck resigned.

Sweatt, Dea. Taylor G., old employee of Amoskeag Co., died Sept. 22, 1894, aged 65.

Sweet, James L., mill overseer, died Feb. 12, 1888, aged 53. An ex-councilman.

System of government formed by delegates at Amherst after flight of Gov. Wentworth in 1775.

Tavern, old Wentworth, Janesville, demolished November, 1889.

Taylor, George M., resident of Manchester since 1846, print-works engraver, died March 23, 1888, aged 68.

Tebbetts & Soule, druggists, stand established 1855.

Telegraph, fire alarm, constructed 1872 at cost of $16,000.

Temperance, Royal Templars of, Granite State council, No. 1, organized Nov. 28, 1878.

Temperance, Sons of, Division No. 3, instituted July 13, 1846; Division No. 8, organized Oct. 26, 1847; Division No. 19, organized 1848; all dissolved by 1852. Manchester division, No. 19, organized Nov. 16, 1860; dissolved May 22, 1863.

Templeton, John, 40 years a resident, died June 9, 1895, aged 77.

Tewksbury, E. Greene, old time bookseller, died March 22, 1877.

Text books, free, system went into effect in grammar schools, Feb. 3, 1890.

Thayer, William E., old resident, died Dec. 27, 1886, aged 61.

Thirty-four out of thirty-six men in Derryfield capable of bearing arms, went to the war on hearing of battle of Lexington.

Time, Standard, adopted by railroads Sept. 10, 1883.

Town divided into highway districts in 1806; districts remained same till 1846.

Town farm voted to be bought, March 12, 1839. Moses Noyes, John Gamble, and James McQueston, committee; $1,000 appropriated in part payment; bought April 22, 1841.

Town-house, first, built in 1842, cost $20,358; burned Aug. 12, 1844.

Town-meeting, first, in Derryfield, held at house of John Hall, tavern-keeper in what is now East Manchester, Sept. 9, 1751.

Town-meeting, special, held to locate meeting-house, favored the Centre, Aug. 13, 1766. Another held December 22 refused to appropriate money to support preaching, but differences were compromised March 2, 1767.

HISTORICAL COMPENDIUM — *Continued.*

Town-meeting, special, held to locate a meeting-house, Sept. 21, 1758. It was to be built on John Hall's land. For several years various votes were passed relating to it. In 1764 it was voted not to raise money for preaching, and the next year the vote was reversed. The meeting-house quarrel continued for years afterwards.

Town-meeting June 5, 1843, authorized the selectmen "to prosecute all persons who may violate the license law," and town liquor agent was appointed.

Town-meeting of 1840 won by people of the "New Town." Amos Weston, Jr., J. T. P. Hunt, and Hiram Brown chosen selectmen.

Town voted in 1803 to petition legislature for permission to build locks on Cohas brook to float lumber from Massabesic lake region, but surrendered work to private individuals in 1806; took five shares of stock in enterprise in 1807, but locks were not built.

Trade, Board of, organized Feb. 5, 1890; rooms, 620, 621 The Kennard.

Treaty of Ghent celebrated at Amoskeag Falls, July 10, 1783, by general merrymaking.

True, George M., former president of common council, died Jan. 19, 1889, aged 35.

Truesdale, John, trunk manufacturer, died Oct. 18, 1891, aged 75.

Trust Co., New Hampshire, begun business Oct. 8, 1885; leased Stark block, Feb. 8, 1892; asked for an injunction, July 24, 1893.

Tubbs, Dr. E. M., died Feb. 7, 1878, aged 54.

Tucker, Rev. William J., ordained Jan. 24, 1867; resigned from Franklin-street Congregational church, Feb. 21, 1875, and closed his labors there in May.

Turnverein, organized 1870; grounds and hall, 265 Turner street.

Tuson, Rocilla M., school teacher, died June 3, 1890, aged 37.

Twiss, Capt. Abram J., Stark overseer, died April 10, 1876, aged 58.

Twombley, John, resident for 50 years, died Dec. 28, 1891, aged 84.

Union, Cigarmakers' International, formed 1882. Meets in St. John's hall, 859 Elm street, second Wednesdays.

Union, St. Pierre, organized 1892.

Union, Union Veterans', Alvin H. Libby, commander; organized December, 1890.

Union, Young Peoples' McCrillis, connected with Universalist church; organized 1885.

United Friends, Order of, Hillsborough council, No. 299; organized January, 1888.

United Order of Pilgrim Fathers:
Webster colony, No. 26, instituted July 5, 1881.

Unity, Manchester, I. O. O. F., Loyal Manchester lodge; instituted April 25, 1891.

Universalist society, Second, formed Dec. 10, 1859; organized as Elm-street Universalist society, Feb. 27, 1867; disbanded 1871.

65

U. O. G. C.:
 Manchester commandery, No. 89, organized Dec. 8, 1879.
 Mizpah commandery, No. 181, organized Feb. 1, 1882.

Valley cemetery accepted Feb. 1, 1841, by vote of 166 to 136.

Varney, David B., elected mayor by 447 plurality, Nov. 5, 1888; republican majority for president, 452; governor, democratic plurality, 5; republican majority for congress, 270.

Varnum, Geo. W., veteran and old resident, died Dec. 13, 1891, aged 73.

Venable, William W., Amoskeag engineer, killed by engine Oct. 19, 1888.

Veterans, Amoskeag, first meeting, Nov. 6, 1854. Hon. Hiram Brown, chairman; Hon. E. E. Patten, clerk. First commander, Col. William P. Riddle. First parade and ball, Feb. 22, 1855. Incorporated Aug. 4, 1855. Visited Boston, Bunker Hill, and Lowell, June, 1855; visited Washington and Mount Vernon, December, 1855.

Veterans, Manchester War, organized March 5, 1870.

Veterans, Sons of, W. W. Brown camp, organized Sept. 23, 1882.

Walker, Josiah, aged resident, died Aug. 12, 1886, aged 75.

Wallace, Rev. Cyrus W., began service as a licentiate of the Londonderry Presbytery at the Amoskeag Congregational church, April, 1839, and was ordained pastor of the First Congregational church, Jan. 8, 1840, being the first minister ordained and installed in town. Resigned Jan. 11, 1873, and resignation was accepted in August. He was identified with church interests for 50 years, first pastor of First Congregational church; died Oct. 21, 1889, aged 84.

Water power of Amoskeag falls averages 10,000 horse-power, with a maximum of 15,000.

Water-works, commission appointed 1844; Manchester Aqueduct Co. chartered 1845; Manchester Aqueduct chartered 1852; another of same name, 1857; City Aqueduct, 1865; surveys made in 1860; another report made by J. B. Sawyer, 1869; committee to examine sources of supply appointed 1871; William J. McAlpine, of Pittsfield, Mass., reported in favor of Massabesic; enabling act passed legislature, June 30, 1871; ordinance passed city council, Aug. 1, 1871; E. A. Straw, E. W. Harrington, William P. Newell, Aretas Blood, Alpheus Gay, A. C. Wallace, appointed commissioners, and they chose S. N. Bell as clerk; J. T. Fanning employed as superintendent; after a public hearing, April, 1872, five voted for Massabesic, one for Burnham's pond, and one for that pond temporarily; work was begun July, 1872, and water was pumped into the city from the lake, July 4, 1874.

Wathen, Rev. Charles B., chosen pastor South Main-street church; installed July 8.

Webster, Daniel, visited Manchester, 1852, and stopped at residence of Richard H. Ayer, corner Central and Chestnut streets, and was given a reception.

Webster, Francis H., 21 years employed on Amoskeag, died April 23, 1895, aged 67.

Webster, Major John, elected first representative from Derryfield and Litchfield, March 25, 1793.

Webster, Dr. William A., surgeon 9th N. H. V., school-master and committee-man, died Feb. 7, 1887, aged 57.

Welch, James, alias "Slasher," murdered John O'Brien, of Milford, March 2, 1895. Got eight years in state prison.

Weston, ex-Gov. James A., banker and financier, died May 8, 1895, aged 67.

Weston, Jason, 30 years employed by Gas Co., clerk in post-office in 1841, later keeper of McGregor bridge toll-gate, died Sept. 6, 1889, aged 84.

Wheat, Dr. Thomas, over 50 years a physician, died March 25, 1895, aged 74.

White, Russell, old resident and business man, died Sept. 1, 1893, aged 73.

Whitford, George, contractor, ex-councilman, etc., died Jan. 4, 1895, aged 59.

Whitman, G. P., appointed agent Amory mill, July 28, 1879.

Whitney, Henry S., came to Manchester in 1836; superintended the cutting of trees where the Amoskeag and Stark tenements now stand; member of fire department and old militia. Died Feb. 28, 1888, aged 80.

Whittemore, David Cophran, horseman and real estate owner, died May 17, 1895, aged 69.

Wilkins, Dr. William W., physician and war veteran, died Sept. 1, 1892, aged 63.

Williams, Charles, nominated for councilor, Oct. 5, 1886.

Williams, George G., 40 years a tailor, died Dec. 5, 1889, aged 66.

Wilson, Thomas, superintendent of dressing in the Stark mills, died Jan. 12, 1875.

Woman's Relief Corps:
Louis Bell, No. 17, organized April 1, 1884.
Joseph Freschl, No. 69, organized July 7, 1891.

"Yellow day," Sept. 6, 1881.

Young, Hiram P., veteran hunter and fireman, died June 12, 1892, aged 57.

Young, John C., old business man, died Oct. 16, 1887, aged 63.

For Free Cuba.

I have arranged to receive contributions for the purchase of medicines and hospital stores for the sick and wounded of the Cuban Patriot Army. Any sum, large or small, will be thankfully received and promptly forwarded.

FRANK H. CHALLIS.

Board of Trade Rooms, The Kennard.

ADDENDA.

Charter, city, accepted Aug. 1, 1846, by vote of 485 to 134.

City auditor's office was established by ordinance, 1889. First incumbent was James B. Straw, who died January, 1894, and was succeeded by James E. Dodge.

City Clerks: John S. T. Cushing, 1846–49; Frederick Smyth, 1849–52; Geo. A. French, 1852–56; Joel Taylor, to April 15, 1856; Frank II. Lyford, 1856–57; Joseph Knowlton, 1857 to his death, May 3, 1865; Joseph E. Bennett, 1865–76; Albert Jackson, 1876; John P. Newell, 1876; Nathan P. Kidder, 1877 to the present time.

Douglass, Stephen A., was in Manchester in 1860, and spoke on Merrimack square.

Eliot, "Apostle to the Indians," is said to have preached in the Indian village which stood where Gov. Smyth's residence, "The Willows," now stands, in 1650.

Elliott, William II., jeweler, established in business September, 1840, on site of present store. His sign has never been absent from Elm street since that date.

Freshet, greatest in memory of "oldest inhabitant," March 2, 1896. West half Granite bridge carried away, also Amoskeag Co.'s foot-bridge and steam-pipe bridge. Water 10.95 feet above Amoskeag dam.

Grain business now conducted by Adams Bros., was founded at its present location in 1849, and the family has been represented in the firm by at least one member ever since.

Grenier, Abraham G., first French Canadian elected to city government, 1883.

Hall, Marshall P., 25 years member of school board, three years city librarian, died Feb. 12, 1896, aged 57.

Kelley's Falls dam swept out Feb. 29, 1896. Electric Co. damaged $50,000.

Kimball, Gilman H., ex-city marshal, tax collector, etc., died Jan. 14, 1874, aged 56.

Kimball & Hobbs, successors to J. Stickney, leather and rubber goods, established in 1852, in basement of Granite block.

Merrill, C. R., flour and grain, "old Depot Store," established 1851.

Partridge Bros., grain dealers, business established 1868.

Wallace, Col. A. C., lumber dealer, established 1843.

ERRATA.

Bridge, Amoskeag, was carried away by a freshet 1853 and rebuilt by the city 1854, not as stated on page 13.

For Watemo Smith, page 50, read Waterman Smith.

Any person discovering an error in fact in this Compendium will confer a favor by calling the attention of the compiler, Frank H. Challis, Board of Trade rooms, to the same.

CITY GOVERNMENT,

1896.

Mayor — WILLIAM C. CLARKE.
City Clerk — NATHAN P. KIDDER.
City Treasurer — FRED L. ALLEN.
Tax Collector — GEORGE E. MORRILL.
City Auditor — JAMES E. DODGE.
City Solicitor — EDWIN F. JONES.
City Engineer — WINFRED H. BENNETT.
City Physician — FREDERICK PERKINS.
City Messenger — JOHN A. BARKER.

ALDERMEN.

Ward 1 — Gardner K. Browning.   Ward 5 — Richard J. Barry.
Ward 2 — George E. Heath.   Ward 6 — Frank H. Libbey.
Ward 3 — George W. Reed.   Ward 7 — Johann A. Graf.
Ward 4 — Howard C. Holt.   Ward 8 — Christian L. Wolf.
Ward 9 — Frank T. Provost.

COMMON COUNCIL.

John T. Gott, President.   George L. Stearns, Clerk.

Ward 1 — Charles E. Blanchard, William Watts, Carl E. Rydin.
Ward 2 — Eben Carr, Ossian D. Knox, John A. Lindquist.
Ward 3 — William F. Elliott, Clarence E. Rose, Joseph O. Tremblay.
Ward 4 — George H. Phinney, George E. Richards, Jules Deschenes.
Ward 5 — William J. Allen, Michael R. Sullivan, Daniel A. Murphy.
Ward 6 — John T. Gott, Charles Hazen, Frank Welch.
Ward 7 — Norris P. Colby, Samuel F. Davis, Robert Morrow.
Ward 8 — Edward F. Scheer, John W. Wilson, William R. Blakely.
Ward 9 — John Gildard, Stephen P. Martel, Robert F. Schindler.

ASSESSORS.

Henry Lewis, John E. Stearns, David O. Furnald, Harrison D. Lord,
George F. Sheehan, George H. Dudley, William T. Rowell, Eugene W.
Brigham, Hermann Wiesner.

SCHOOL COMMITTEE.

Ward 1 — Walter B. Heath, C. Lambert.
Ward 2 — Augustus P. Horne, Charles H. Manning.
Ward 3 — George D. Towne, Louis E. Phelps.
Ward 4 — Charles M. Floyd, Nathaniel L. Colby.
Ward 5 — James P. Slattery, Harry J. Woods.

Ward 6 — Harry I. Dodge, Herbert E. Richardson.
Ward 7 — Fred W. Pillsbury, Edward B. Woodbury.
Ward 8 — Luther C. Baldwin, Josiah G. Dearborn.
Ward 9 — Robert E. Walsh, Jeremiah Sullivan.

William C. Clarke, *ex-officio*, Chairman.
John T. Gott, *ex-officio*.
Marshall P. Hall, Vice-Chairman.
Edward B. Woodbury, Clerk.
William E. Buck, Superintendent Public Instruction.
Curtis W. Davis, Truant Officer.

POLICE DEPARTMENT.

Court.

Isaac L. Heath, Justice. George W. Prescott, Special Justice.
John C. Bickford, Clerk.

Commissioners.

Harry E. Loveren, Chairman; Noah S. Clark, Clerk; Frank P. Carpenter.

Officers.

Michael J. Healy, Chief of Police.
John F. Cassidy, Deputy Chief of Police.
Thomas E. Steele, Sergeant.
Levi J. Proctor, Captain of Night Watch.

FIRE ENGINEERS.

Thomas W. Lane, Chief; Fred S. Bean, Clerk; Ruel G. Manning, Eugene S. Whitney, Clarence R. Merrill.

STREET AND PARK DEPARTMENT.

Commissioners.

George H. Stearns, Chairman; L. P. Reynolds, H. P. Simpson; Allen E. Herrick, Clerk; Julia F. Stearns, Assistant Clerk.

Agents.

CITY LIBRARY.

Trustees — Frank P. Carpenter, Nathan P. Hunt, Herman F. Straw, Walter M. Parker, Isaac W. Smith, Moody Currier, Charles D. McDuffie. William C. Clarke, John T. Gott, *ex-officio*. Kate E. Sanborn, Librarian.

SINKING FUND COMMISSIONERS.

Alpheus Gay, George H. Stearns, Fred L. Allen.

BOARD OF HEALTH.

Office in County Court House.

Cornelius F. Starr, M. D., William K. Robbins, Clarence W. Downing, M. D.; Cornelius F. Starr, President; William K. Robbins, Secretary; Herbert S. Clough, John F. Looney, Sanitary Inspectors; Richard J. Barry, Plumbing Inspector.

OVERSEERS OF THE POOR.

Meet third Wednesday of each month.

William H. Maxwell, Thomas L. Quimby, Benjamin F. Garland, George S. Holmes, Patrick Costello, Charles Francis, William Marshall, Charles S. McKean, Moise Bessette; William C. Clarke, *ex-officio*, Chairman; William H. Maxwell, Clerk.

CITY FARM.

Eugene G. Libby, Superintendent.   Mrs. Eugene G. Libby, Matron.

City Weigher — Asa B. Eaton.
Sealer of Weights and Measures — Harry C. Blanchard.
Milk Inspector — Edward C. Smith.
Inspectors of Petroleum — John Cayzer, Joseph B. Baril.

INSPECTORS OF CHECK-LISTS.

George C. Kemp, Charles B. Tucker, William B. Corey, Samuel J. Lord, Patrick E. Daly, Albert J. Peaslee, Joseph A. Foster, Charles C. Tinkham, John B. Bourque.

TRUSTEES OF CEMETERIES.

Four Years — John F. Frost, William H. Huse; Three Years — John L. Sanborn, Bushrod W. Hill; Two Years — Stillman P. Cannon, James E. Bailey; One Year — Edwin F. Jones, John P. Young. Fred L. Allen, Clerk.

Sub-Trustees of Cemeteries.

Pine Grove — Alderman Graf; Councilman Blanchard; Messrs. Frost, Jones, and Young. Edwin F. Jones, Clerk.
Valley — Alderman Holt; Councilman Gildard; Messrs. Sanborn, Hill, and Cannon. Stillman P. Cannon, Clerk.
Amoskeag — Councilman Carr; Messrs. Huse and Bailey.

Byron A. Stearns, Superintendent Pine Grove Cemetery.
Charles H. G. Foss, Superintendent Valley Cemetery.
James E. Bailey, Superintendent Amoskeag Cemetery.

Trustees Cemetery Funds.

Charles H. Bartlett, Otis Barton; William C. Clarke, Chairman, *ex-officio*.

71

MANCHESTER BUSINESS — 1896.

Advertiser.

Frank H. Challis. Board of Trade Rooms

Apothecaries.

John L. Beaudry & Co. 1023 Elm
Brien & Moquin, 1160 Elm
J. Oscar Burbank, 635 Elm
Z. F. CAMPBELL, 955 Elm
N. H. Colby, 1231 Elm
Edward H. Currier, 782 Elm
G. L. D. Martigny, 589 Elm
J. F. Dignam & Co. 797 Elm
Joseph Doucet & Co., Main cor. Wayne
Charles E. Dufort, 687 Elm
Eames Bros. 1089 Elm
John B. Hall, 1029 Elm
John J. Holland, 893 Elm
Frank A. James, 1213 Elm
Littlefield Drug Co. 1133 Elm
MARSHALL & KNOWLTON, 744 Elm and Lowell cor. Nashua
WALTER B. MITCHELL, 344 Granite
FRANCIS C. MIVILLE. 535 Main
Potvin & Co.. Amory cor. McGregor
Albert J. Precourt, Central cor. Chestnut
George E. Richards & Co. 1104 Elm
Roy & Boire Drug Co. 1129 Elm
CHARLES E. SILVER, 405 East Spruce
Amasa D. Smith, 142 Merrimack
E. C. Smith, 1277 Elm
SNELLING & WOODS, 1167 Elm
TEBBETTS & SOULE, 786 Elm
Fred H. Thurston, 879 Elm
FRANK L. WAY, 24 South Main
C. A. Williams, Lake ave. cor. Hall
C. J. Woods & Co. 138 Lake ave
HENRY A. ZICKENDRATH, 134 School

Architects.

BARTLETT & GAY, 852 Elm, room 19
WILLIAM M. BUTTERFIELD, 1008 Elm, room 608
CHICKERING & O'CONNELL, 1037 Elm, rooms 18 and 19

Auctioneers.

CAVANAUGH BROS. 46 to 48 West Central
Henry B. Fairbanks, 54 and 58 Hanover

Bakers.

Philias Archambeault, 225 Putnam
E. R. Barry, 85 Hanover
John Bergmann, 95 Manchester
Wesley Bernhardt, 61 Hanover
Bourassa Bros. 570 Elm
A. C. Brember, 24 Boynton
William Carroll, 60 Lake ave
Cote & Son, 471 Main
Michael Cronin, 80 Lake ave
Alcide Demers, Amory cor. Alsace
Ludger Desrochers, 89 Manchester
L. H. Gauvin, 39 Central
CARL KOEHLER & SON, 977 Elm and 38 South Main
Gustav Kretschmar, 92 Second
WILLIAM D. LADD & CO. 1208 Elm
Lindquist Bros. 20 Concord
McQUADE'S General Store, 607 Elm
Mary McQuillan, 131 Central
A. A. Nerbonne & Co. 85 Nashua
New York Pie Bakery, 841 Union
A. Rivard, 68 Lowell
Standard Bread Co. 61 Hanover
Andrew Sym, 653 Elm
Amedee Tribaudeau, 29 Pearl
Henry J. Wood, 215 Hanover

Banks.

Amoskeag National, 867 Elm
AMOSKEAG SAVINGS, 867 Elm
BANK OF NEW ENGLAND, Elm cor. Hanover
FIRST NATIONAL, 1028 Elm
Guaranty Savings, Elm cor. Manchester
Manchester National, 902 Elm
MANCHESTER SAVINGS, 902 Elm
Mechanics Savings, 992 Elm
Merchants National, Elm cor. Manchester
Merrimack River Savings, 1028 Elm
New Hampshire Trust Co. 994 Elm
Peoples Savings, 867 Elm
Second National, 992 Elm

Barrel Dealer.

ALBERT MOULTON, 28 to 58 Winter

Beef Dealers.

CHARLES E. COX, 36 Granite
Manchester Beef Co., Franklin cor. West Cedar
Nelson, Morris & Co. 174 Franklin
Warren K. Richardson, Goffstown road (A)

Bicycle Dealers.

G. F. HOWE & CO, 1038 Elm
MANCHESTER HEATING AND LIGHTING CO. 1082 Elm
B. R. WHEELER, 127 Hanover

Bobbin Manufacturer.

JAMES BALDWIN CO., Mast St., W. M.

Booksellers and Stationers.

E. R. COBURN CO. 866 Elm
W. P. Goodman, 41 Hanover
Josephine M. LeBoeuf, 1111 Elm
Lloyd T. Meade, 12 to 14 Hanover
Temple & Farrington Co. 907 to 911 Elm
PIPER & McINTIRE, 1059 Elm

Boot and Shoe Dealers.

Francois H. Auger, 1144 Elm
Beauchemin & Quirin, 1057 Elm
Arthur T. Beaumier, 521 Main
Bolander & Swanson 1355 Elm
Burke Bros. 917 Elm
John Cashman, 30 Church
William H. Cate, 67 Hanover
John Cayzer, 140 School
Costello Bros. 1118 Elm
Edward P. Cronan, 162 Manchester
Napoleon Daigle, 118 Manchester
George W. Dodge, 931 Elm
Dodge & Straw, 1011 Elm
F. C. Dow. 888 Elm
WILLIAM P. FARMER, 750 Elm
Simon Feldman, 651 Elm
John Francis, 1209 Elm
Charles L. Fuller, 60 Massabesic
A. and W. S. Heath, 817 Elm
J. A. Labrecque, 1151 Elm
J. R. Laflamme & Co. 16 Hanover
Lightbody & Burbank, 861 Elm
Montplaisir & Fowler, 1187 Elm
Narcisse O. Morin & Co. 1115 Elm
T. J. O'Connor, 34 Merrimack
Parent & Trudeau, 37 Marion
GEORGE L. ROBINSON, 348 Granite
Scheer & Renker, 58 South Main
Daniel F. Shea, 790 Elm
Harris Simon, 643 Elm
C. H. Thayer & Co. 971 Elm
Patrick F. Toole, 547 Elm
Frank Vytal, 686 Elm
Francis Whitman, 12 Main
Wingate & Gould, 947 Elm

Boot and Shoe Findings.

Daniel W. Osgood, 646 Elm
KIMBALL & HOBBS, 1064 to 1068 Elm

Boot and Shoe Manufacturers.

Crafts & Green, West Hancock cor. Second
Eaton Heights Shoe Co. Page
Eureka Shoe Co., Lincoln cor. Silver
F. M. Hoyt & Co., Lincoln cor. Silver
E. A. Jennings & Co. 343 Kelley
Kimball Bros. Shoe Co., Massabesic cor. Cypress
Redman & Eaton Shoe Co., W. Hancock below Second

Bottlers.

W. A. Burroughs, 192, 194 Merrimack
James E. Gallagher, 329 Pine
THOMAS F. CLANCY, 542 Elm
William F. Glancy, 548 Elm
P. Harrington, 17 Lake ave.
Hinckel Brewing Co. 365 Elm
Howe & Streeter, rear 672 Elm
Robert Schneider, 44 Ferry
Edward Wagner, 32 Manchester
John G. Wagner, 205 Second

Building and Loan Associations.

Citizens' Building & Loan Association, 883 Elm
Granite State Provident Association, 1008 Elm
Manchester Building & Loan Association, 619 The Kennard

Business Colleges.

Bryant & Stratton Business College, 827 Elm
Daniels & Downs, Pickering block

Carpenters and Builders.

LYMAN M. ALDRICH, 112 Manchester
C. W. Atwood, 319 East Spruce
Arthur L. Bixby, 78 Manchester
Bixby & Wilson, 51 Riddle
William Carr, 394 Concord
George A. Clarke, 1338 Elm
Charles H. Colburn, 294 Laurel
Dana & Provost, 21 Amory & 41 Union
George H. Dudley, 159 Laurel
Flint & Lewis, Birch near Lowell
E. Gatz & Graupner, 4 West Auburn
Frank M. Goings, 782 Summer
HEAD & DOWST CO. 97 Granite
S. L. Higgins, 380 Pearl
George Holbrook, 127 Manchester
E. A. G. Holmes, rear 224 Manchester
Frank X. Laflamme, 387 Belmont
Henry F. W. Little, rear 13 Lowell
Mead, Mason & Co. 219 Concord
James H. Mendell & Co., The Kennard
David G. Mills, 44 North Main
Walter Neal, 310 Hanover
Ernest Veasey, 283 Concord
SANBORN T. WORTHEN, The Kennard

Carriage Manufacturers and Dealers.

JOHN T. BEACH, 516 Elm
James Benson, Candia road at Massabecic
Edgar E. Brown, Central cor. Cass
John F. Conway, 107 Merrimack
Couch & McDonald, East Spruce cor. Belmont
GEORGE S. EASTMAN, 127 South Main
A. FILION, 19 Fourth
Kimball Carriage Co. 88 West Central
J. B. McCrillis & Son, Bridge cor. Malvern
Ludger Paris, 162 Front (A)
Sanborn Carriage Co., Chestnut cor. Lowell
Charles J. Shanessy, 160 South Main

Cigar Dealers and Manufacturers.

F. A. Barrett, West Manchester
P. J. Clancey, 98 Jewett
William G. Connor, 949 Elm
Joseph Demers & Co. 154 McGregor
Samuel F. Doran, 18 Manchester
James H. Dwyer, 663 Elm
John Eaton, 1069 Elm
Simon Fleischman, 97 Hanover
T. J. Foley & Co. 917 Elm
D. F. Griffin, 74 Manchester
George H. Hubbard, 8 to 10 Hanover
John McDerby, 20 Main
LEONARD P. REYNOLDS, 724 Elm
Robinson Bros. 3 Dean ave.
Leon Saidel, 1101 Elm
Max Schwatzer, 165 South Main
Ferdinand G. Seelig, 28 Manchester
Isaac Siegel, 1195 Elm
ROGER G. SULLIVAN, 803 Elm and 66 West Central
T. F. Sullivan, 981 Elm and 231 Granite
James S. Washburn, 56 Massabesic
Lewis W. Whitney, 1 Dean ave.

Civil Engineers.

George H. Allen, 924 Elm
BARTLETT & GAY, 852 Elm, room 19
Winfred H. Bennett, City Engineer's office
Perry H. Dow, Amoskeag Manufacturing Co.
Henry A. Herrick, 912 Elm
Charles S. Kidder, Union, above Clark
Joseph P. Sawyer, 936 Elm
Charles K. Walker, Court House building
John P. Young, Hanover, opp. Page

Clothing and Furnishing Goods.

Amoskeag Clothing Co. 1045 Elm
Cushman & Hardy Co. 844 to 848 Elm
C. M. Floyd & Co. 831 Elm
Hoffman Bros. 898 Elm
Bernard Kamber, 671 Elm

Mrs. B. Kearns, 506 Elm
Frank P. Kimball, 1053 to 1055 Elm
Lane & Dozois, 1005 Elm
William Marcotte & Co. 963 to 965 Elm
McELROY & WATHEN, 951 Elm, room 3
Herbert M. Moody, 950 Elm
Michael O'Dowd, 922 Elm
Plumer & Holton, 895 to 899 Elm
William Shretski, 1045 Elm
Sullivan & Custen, 1140 and 1163 Elm
Alonzo Tarbell, 970 Elm
Weston & Martin, 836 Elm

Coal and Wood.

L. B. BODWELL & Co. 640 Elm
William H. Bourassa, 358 Pine
J. B. Cate, 118 Massabesic
John J. Cushing, 107 Merrimack
M. Desfosses & Son, 33 Pearl
W. E. Dunbar & Son, Massabesic
DUNLAP & WASON COAL Co. 668 Elm
A. H. Girardin, 251 East High
Frank Graveline, 42 Cedar
Manchester Coal and Ice Co. 1164 Elm
Joseph Masse, 1116 Elm
Archibald McIndoe, rear 18 Lake ave.
Moore & Preston, 1308 Elm
Louis Mueller, 93 Frederick
John H. Parmerton, 40 West Central
Petterson & Lindquist, 1272 Elm
D. M. POORE, 684 Elm
E. W. POORE, 678 Elm
W. E. Prescott, 81 Central
J. P. Russell & Co, 558 Elm
August Schirk, 213 Second
E. V. Turcotte, 196 Manchester
Wilson & McKee, 38 Massabesic
James F. Wyman, 85 South Main

Concrete Pavement.

Charles H. Robie Concrete Co., 936 Elm
Jonathan T. Underhill, The Kennard

Confectionery, Fruit, Etc.

E. R. Barry, 85 Hanover
Louis Belli, 802 Elm
Ephraim Booth, 109 Hanover
Andrew Bruno & Co. 639 Elm
John H. Canney, 410 Massabesic
John Delorme, 108 Manchester
Joseph Ferrari, 690 Elm
Joseph Ferretti, 1163 Elm
Thomas Kelley, 1073 and 1201 Elm
CARL C. KOEHLER & SON, 977 Elm
Charles Langmaid, 114 Central and 519 Lincoln
Mrs. J. F. McCarty, 54 Merrimack
George A. Murphy, 1070 Elm
Patrick J. Connell, 376 Chestnut
M. Padovani & Co, 89 Hanover
J. Piller & Co, 740 Elm
J. D. Rouse, 624 Elm

Max Saidel, 87 Central
Charles Tootinglan, 111 Manchester
Henry H. Travis, 1265 Elm

Copper, Tin and Iron Roofing.

H. J. LAWSON, 53 Lowell

Cotton Goods Manufactories.

Amory Manufacturing Co. Canal cor. West Bridge
Amoskeag Manufacturing Co. Canal foot Stark
Jefferson Mills, foot of Dean
Manchester Mills Manufacturing Co. foot West Central
Manchester Print Works, State cor. Granite
Stark Mills, Canal foot Mechanic

Counselors.

Andrews & Andrews, 623 and 624 Kennard
Charles H. Bartlett, 27 Opera House block
John P. Bartlett, 1 and 2 Opera House block
JOHN C. BICKFORD, 885 Elm, room 2
Henry W. Blair, 19 Opera House block
Oliver E. Branch, 924 Elm
James F. Briggs, 1 Patten's block, 924 Elm
BURNHAM, BROWN & WARREN, 605 The Kennard
WILLIAM G. BUTEAU, 314 The Kennard
John W. Center, 36 Opera House block
Charles E. Cochran, 924 Elm
Nathaniel W. Colby, 886 Elm
John G. Crawford, 859 Elm
David Cross, 936 Elm
Joseph Dearborn, 157 Milford
Drury & Peaslee, 614 The Kennard
Joseph W. Fellows, 859 Elm
John Foster, 852 Elm
William S. Franklin, 1008 Elm
John Gage, 839 Elm
Isaac L. Heath, 924 Elm
Timothy J. Howard, 936 Elm
Nathan P. Hunt, 924 Elm
Edwin F. Jones, 924 Elm
Joseph Le Boeuf, 1111 Elm
FRANK C. LIVINGSTON, 859 Elm, room 7
Harry T. Lord, 896 Elm
Harry E. Loveren, 936 Elm
George I. McAllister, 20 Hanover
John T. Moore, 896 Elm
Morgan & Boisvert, 301 and 302 The Kennard
O'Connor & Shea, 20 Opera House block
Thomas J. O'Donnell, 924 Elm
John O'Neill, 8 and 9 Opera House block
Alpheus C. Osgood, 859 Elm

PATTEE & GEORGE, 312 and 313 The Kennard
David L. Perkins, 896 Elm
D. P. Perkins, 163 Concord
George W. Prescott, 924 Elm
John H. Riedell, 323 The Kennard
ISAAC W. SMITH, 330 to 331 The Kennard
P. H. Sullivan, 2 and 3 Opera House block
Sulloway & Topliff, 22 and 23 Opera House block
David A. Taggart, 936 Elm
EMILE H. TARDIVEL, 524 to 526 The Kennard
James P. Tuttle, 27 Opera House block
Gordon Woodbury, 886 Elm

Dentists.

F. H. Bachelder, 852 Elm
H. Baldwin & Son, 1061 Elm
Blackstone & Fisher, 929 Elm
Boston Dental Parlors, 1061 Elm
Clarence W. Buck, 788 Elm
FRANK C. CHASE, 852 Elm
William F. Childs, Hanover, near Merrimack
C. W. CLEMENT, 336 The Kennard
Bruno R. Desrosiers, 1152 Elm
C. S. Eklund, 1087 Elm
Charles L. Fitzpatrick, 22 Concord
N. T. Folsom, 59 Dover
Hiram Hill, 327 Manchester
Orlando H. Johnson, The Kennard
Henry W. Loxton, 336 Granite
William E. Marden, 48 Hanover
Charles E. Page, 1017 Elm
John J. Pepin, 801 Elm
John R. Prescott, 794 Elm
Edwin A. Quinn, 942 Elm
Edward W. Rowe, 951 Elm
Andrew J. Sawyer, 436 The Kennard
Charles W. Tobin, 141 Cedar

Dining Rooms.

E. R. Parry, 85 Hanover
BARTLETT & WEED, Union Dining Rooms, 89 Hanover
Billerica House Dining Rooms, Chestnut, cor. Hanover
Harriet Champaigne, 1272 Elm
C. E. Clough, Merrimack, cor. Elm
A. E. Cooley, 1122 Elm
P. H. Cuddy, 18 Lake ave.
Dan Davis, 22 Manchester
Diet Kitchen, 45 Central
CARL C. KOEHLER & SON, 977 Elm
A. E. Martyn, Star Coffee House cor. Stark and Elm
Gem Lunch Rooms, 60 West Central
Laurel House, 297 Chestnut
Frank I. Page, Elm, cor. Mechanic
N. F. Perkins, 13 Concord
Queen City Lunch Rooms, 16½ Hanover

Standard Bread Co., W. Bernhardt
  Proprietor, 61 Hanover
The Bedford Dining Room, 1371 Elm
James Watts & Co, 2 Manchester
William Wells, 119 Merrimack

Dry Goods.

Barton & Co. 849 to 853 Elm
Caldwell Sisters, 340 Granite
Mrs. Denise Chalifoux, 34 Marion
Charles Cote, 517 Main
Desaulniers & Co. 531 Main
Gazille & Co, 25 Hanover
Patrick Kean, 45 Hanover
Leonidas P. Labonte, 855 to 857 Elm
Frank W. Leeman, 37 Lowell
Mrs. M. A. McDonough, 543 Elm
Miville & Deschenes, 889 to 891 Elm
New York Store Branch, 6 Main
Sarah R. Nickles 1375 Elm
Paris Bros., 995 Elm
John Robbie Co. 868 to 884 Elm
GEORGE H. TANSWELL, 39 Hanover
Patrick F. Toole, 547 Elm
Trahan & Co. 491 North Main
E. C. Wescott. 24 Hanover
Weston & Hill Co., Elm cor. Merrimack

Dyers and Scourers.

Ankarloo Steam Dye House, 23 Depot
A. M. Goodwin, 69 Manchester
HEATON & SON, 179 South Main &
  1212 Elm

Electric Light Co.

Ben Franklin Electric Light Co. 42
  Hanover
MANCHESTER ELECTRIC LIGHT
  CO. 42 Hanover
Union Electric Co. 34 Market

Fancy Goods.

Bee Hive 937 to 941 Elm
S. E. Butterfield ,1303 Elm
Clark & Estey 19 Hanover
Frank W. Fitts, 9 to 13 Hanover
S. G. Fletcher 962 Elm
Lizzie Gillis 1199 Elm
Hardy & Folsom 863 Elm
Maggie J. McAllister, 1179 Elm Rooms
  1 & 2
Mrs. M. A. McDonough, 543 Elm
Nadeau & Pierre, 1085 Elm
S. R. Nickles 1375 Elm
George A. Parsons, 1171 Elm
Mrs. J. J. Stanton.110 Central
F. S. Young, 990 Elm

Electricians.

Brodie Electric Co, 886 Elm
E. M. Bryant, 8 Market
Harrison Corey, 1043 Elm

MANCHESTER HEATING AND
  LIGHTING CO, 1082 Elm
Perkins & Franks.1043 Elm
J. Brodie Smith, 142 Merrimack

Engravers.

Paige & Myrick.896 Elm
W. H. SHILVOCK, 143 Hanover

Express Offices.

American Express Co. 860 Elm
John D. Blake, (Deerfield) 860 Elm
Goffstown Express 809 Elm
Manchester & Concord Express Co.
  36 Hanover

Fish and Oysters.

Charles T. Allen, 13 Lowell
Hall & Stearns. 309 Pine
Thomas E. McDerby, 573 Elm
Elvin S. Newton, 96 Manchester

Florists.

A. G. Hood, 238 Pearl
H. H. Huntress, 101 Boynton
James Kirby, 71 Oak
Frank A. Koerner, 228 Main
Louis B. Schwarz, Old Mast Road &
  Rockland ave.
RAY BROOK GARDEN CO, 30 Hanover
Frederick S. Worthen & Son, 112 Milford

Flour, Grain, Meal, and Feed.

ADAMS BROS, 754 Elm
Annis Flour & Grain Co, Pine cor.
  Valley
W. M. Avery & Co, 265 Pine
S. L. Flanders, 229 Front (A)
FREEMAN & MERRILL 405 Elm
A. H. Girardin, 251 East High
CLARENCE R. MERRILL, 72 to 90
  Granite
Henry W. Parker, 30 Granite
PARTRIDGE BROS. 1258 Elm
Piscataquog Steam Flour & Grain
  Mills, 120 South Main
Wilson & McKee, 58 Massabesic

Furniture Dealers, Manufacturers and Upholsterers.

M. C. Blanchard & Co., rear 566 Elm
Mrs. Odile Caron, 1203 Elm
W. A. Dakin & Co. 1054 Elm
A. DeMoulpied, 1165 and 1167 Elm
CHARLES De MOULPIED & CO.
  19 to 23 Lake avenue
H. B. Fairbanks, 54 to 58 Hanover
A. M. Finney, 21 Hanover
B. D. Gay, 72 Hanover
C. A. Hoitt & Co., 820 Elm

Josselyn & Read Co., Franklin cor. West Auburn
James P. Martin, 710 Elm
Charles S. McKean, 168 South Main
J. Y. McQueston Co. 652 to 656 Elm
NEW HAMPSHIRE FURNITURE STORE, 1020 Elm
Darwin A. Simons, 1044 to 1048 Elm
Syndicate Furniture Co. 1097 Elm

Gas Co.

PEOPLES' GAS LIGHT CO. 46 Hanover

Granite and Marble Workers.

Charles A. Bailey, rear 325 Elm
George F. Bond, Union and Valley
PALMER & GARMON, 604 Elm
Charles A. Stewart, Milford
R. P. Stevens & Co., 113 Hanover

Grocers Wholesale.

I. W. Monroe, 56 Granite
Henry W. Parker, 30 Granite
John H. Parmerton, 40 to 42 West Central

Grocers Retail.

M. E. Alton, 49 Massabesic
Philias Archambeault, 225 Putnam
Mrs. M. W. Avery, 265 Pine
Barlow & Nye, 71 Hanover
Willie F. Bean, 45 Ashland
Beauchemin & Pariseau, 1284 Elm
E. Beausejour, 95 Central
Jean B. Belanger, 55 Lake avenue
Bienvenue & Turcotte, 87 Amherst and 134 Front (A)
F. J. Bixby, 726 Elm
Blake & Beadle, 367 Massabesic
Boone & Gates, Pearl cor. Hall
Napoleon Bournival, 677 Valley
E. Lewis Bryant, 1191 Elm
John F. Cahill, 443 Main
John Cashman, 30 Church
Arthur H. Cate, 653 Chestnut
A. N. Charpentier, 28 Concord
A. N. CLAPP, 354 Granite
Charles H. Clark, 352 Amherst
JOHN W. CLAY, 312 Lake avenue
Napoleon Daigle, 122 Manchester
George W. Davis, 456 South Main
E. P. Desrochers, 34 Bridge
Benjamin F. Dickinson, 420 Manchester
EAGER & CO. 776 Elm
Arthur M. Eastman, 119 Hanover
Edgar C. Eastman, 872 Valley
H. I. Faucher, 1117 Elm
Tilton F. Fifield, 57 Hanover
Sherman L. Flanders, 229 Front (A)
H. FRADD & CO. 350 Main cor. Granite
GEORGE E. FRENCH, corner Granite and Main

Alfred L. Gadbois, 1286 and 1288 Elm
Gelinas & Voyer, 90 Concord
J. L. D. Gamache & Co. 20 and 22 Lake avenue
P. C. Gamache & Co. 50 Lake avenue
Granite State Grocery Co. 298 Pine
Alvah H. Gray, 4 Derry
ABRAHAM G. GRENIER, 1156 Elm
P. F. Grenier, 71 Manchester
Griffin Bros. 593 Elm
Hall & Stearns, 309 Pine
P. Harrington, 79 Cedar
Mary A. Hastings, 43 Birch
James Hayes, 18 Cedar
Mary Hayes, 175 Cedar
Reinhardt Hecker, 232 Douglas
Horace J. Holmes, 1321 and 1325 Elm
Evariste Houle, 412 Amory
Joseph Huard, 453 Main
John A. Kane, 45 Brown avenue
O. D. KNOX & CO. 1244 and 1252 Elm
T. J. Labrecque, 1232 Elm
Joseph N. Lacourse & Co. 167 Manchester
Lamoureux Bros. 132 School
Albert Lemire, 26 Marion
Lindquist Bros. 20 Concord
George C. Lord, 224 Lowell
C. S. Magoon & Co. 401 East Spruce
Thomas H. Mahoney, 110 East Spruce
E. Marchand, 50 Amory
Antoine Marcouiller, 187 Manchester
Philip Martel, 238 Wilson
Pierre Martin, 32 Pearl
Martin McIntire, 56 Spruce
McQUADE'S GENERAL STORE, 607 Elm
Monette & Newcombe, 563 Elm
Edward F. Murray, Lake avenue cor. Union
Albert N. Nettle, Goff's Falls
NOYES & PRINCE, Mast cor. South Main
Albert Oliver, 222 Putnam
Parnell Bros. 77 Nashua
Edward W. Perkins, 1217 Elm
Edmond Picard, 1157 to 1159 Elm
Darwin M. Poore & Son, 1139 Elm
O. W. Price, 29 Nashua
Public Market & Packing Co., Franklin and West Central
EUGENE QUIRIN, 501 to 507 Main
George Roe, 290 Belmont
Mary Readon, 66 Cedar
N. B. Reed, Candia road
Ferdinand Riedel, 53 Walker
Charles Robitaille, 101 Manchester
Morris Sack, 402 Union
Scheer & Renker, 54 to 58 South Main
D. A. Shanahan, 38 Lake ave.
Steele & Flanders, 815 Chestnut
Traban & Co. 491 Main
J. N. TUCK & Co. 1060 Elm
Octave J. Turcotte, 588 to 592 Elm
J. J. Twomey, 91 Cedar

Moses Verrette, 609 to 613 Elm
Noe Verrette, 127 Beech
Calixte Vigneault, 133 Merrimack
Henry Weber, 183 Second
J. H. WIGGIN & Co. 923 to 925 Elm
Herbert H. Williams. Summer Cor.
   Massabesic
Samuel M. Worthley, 445 Lake ave.
William D. Young, 1351 Elm

Hardware.

Manchester Hardware Co. 938 Elm
John E. Varick Co, 869 to 813 Elm
Wadleigh Hardware Co. 1601 Elm
J. H. Wilson, Jr. 525 Main West Manchester

Harness Makers, Horse Clothing, Etc.

William H. Adams, Jr. 370 Chestnut
Fred Allen Co. 1202 Elm
Noe Blanchette, 33 Pearl
George Dunnington, 46 Manchester
GEORGE S. EASTMAN, 127 South
   Main
William E. Greeley, Lake ave. cor.
   Massabesic
John F. Kerwin, 45 West Central
Kimball Carriage Co. 88 West Central
RANNO HARNESS Co. 169 South
   Main
Thomas P. Riley, 576 Elm
Peter D. St. Germain, 133 Manchester
N. J. WHALEN, 99 to 101 Merrimack
Ivory S. York, 1326 to 1330 Elm

Hairworkers.

GEORGE W. PETTIGREW, 120
   Bridge
Calvin L. Walker, 915½ Elm

Horse Dealers.

CAVANAUGH BROS. 46 to 48 West
   Central

Hosiery Manufacturers.

Elliott Manufacturing Co., Wilson cor.
   Valley
A. P. Olzendam Hosiery Co., South
   Manchester Mills
Harry P. Ray, at Industrial school

Hotels

Amoskeag Hotel, 270 Front St. (A)
Billerica House, 121 Hanover
Central House, 788 Elm
City Hotel, 1102 Elm
Edwards House, 69 Hanover
Elm House, 724 Elm
Glenwood House, 752 Elm
Hotel Canadian, 597 Elm
Hotel Kimball, 496 to 498 Elm
Hotel Merrimack, 13 to 19 South Main
HOTEL OXFORD, 610 to 620 Elm

Lake View House, Candia road, near
   Auburn line
Lowell St. House, 43 Lowell
Massabesic Hotel, Massabesic Lake
Mill Dam House, Island Pond road
New City Hotel, 1128 to 1138 Elm
New Manchester House, 32 Merrimack
Vining's Hotel, 772 Elm
Webster House, 1306 Elm

Ice Dealers.

L. B. BODWELL & CO. 640 Elm
Manchester Coal and Ice Co. 1164 Elm
A. D. Maxwell, 1308 Elm
Stearns Brothers, 421 Front street (A)

Insurance Agents.

Henry Briggs, 913 Elm
William A. Burgess, 913 Elm
J. F. Chase, 10 Amherst
CHENEY & CHENEY, 999 Elm
   rooms 5, 6 and 9
CLOUGH & TWOMBLY, 886 Elm
JOHN J. DILLON, 300 and 303 The
   Kennard
Dow & Burnham, 29 Pembroke building
John Dowst, 97 Granite
CLARENCE M. EDGERLY, 14 Market
Alfred Ela, 1061 Elm
A. ELLIOTT & CO. 883 Elm
Everett & Smith, 936 Elm
JAMES A. FOLSOM, 1 Pembroke
   block
John C. French, 876 Elm
W. H. GOGGIN, 839 Elm
CHARLES C. HAYES, 339 The Kennard
D. J. Jones, 883 Elm
Paul V. Labonte, 1037 Elm
N. H. Lander, 29 Pembroke block
A. J. Lane Co. 856 Elm
JOHN G. LANE, 64 Hanover
Dugrenier, Lor & Co. 309 The Kennard
Martin & Edgerly, 987 Elm
JOSEPH S. MASSECK, 77 Hanover
W. H. Moison, 310 The Kennard
John T. Moore, 896 Elm
Walter M. Morgan, 300 The Kennard
Harry A. Piper, 886 Elm
EDWIN P. RICHARDSON, 839 Elm
John A. Sheehan, 913 Elm
Stark & Blanchet, 987 Elm
S. B. STEARNS, 4 Pembroke building
William T. Stevens, 991 Elm
George W. Weeks, 970 Elm
James A. Wellman, 913 Elm

Intelligence Offices.

H. H. Dustin, 924 Elm, room 3
JAMES A. FOLSOM, 1 Pembroke
   building
J. S. MASSECK, 77 Hanover

Jewelers.

CARL W. ANDERSON & CO. 894 Elm
J. B. Chasse, 485 Main
DUMAS BROTHERS, 1241 Elm
J. Geoffrion, 613 Elm,
G. F. HOWE & CO. 1078 Elm
L. KIRSCH, 95 Hanover
H. I. Lemay, 1083 Elm
Lovejoy & Stratton. 892 Elm
John Mooar, 940 Elm
E. Pontaut, 1148 Elm
Forrest F. Shaw, 989 Elm
James P. Slattery. 823 Elm
John Taylor, 45 South Main
Charles Thompson. 348 Granite
C. A. Trefethen. 959 Elm
Fred Watts, 990 Elm

Laundries.

GEORGE CLAIR, North End Hand
   Laundry, 1361 Elm
John P. Connors, 20 West Central
Charles W. Goodwin. rear 414 Belmont
C. S. James. 25 Bridge
Walter B. James. 1216 Elm
Laport & Carpenter. 51 South Main
Manchester Steam Laundry, 116
   Franklin
People's Steam Laundry. 403 East
   Spruce
Richardson & Geisel, 137 Hanover
James E. Smith. 330 Granite
Troy Steam Laundry, rear 250 Concord

Leather and Rubber Goods.

KIMBALL & HOBBS. 1064 to 1068
   Elm

Library.

City Library and Reading room.
   Franklin and Market

Lumber Dealers.

Gilman Clough. 24 Manchester
Lewis A. Clough. 24 Manchester
Dana & Provost. 41 Union and 21
   Amory
S. C. FORSAITH MACHINE CO..
   foot of West Auburn
HEAD & DOWST CO. 97 Granite
J. Hodge, 485 Elm
Albert J. Sawyer, West Auburn cor.
   Franklin
A. C. Wallace, 168 South Main

Machinists.

George A. Farwell, 92 West Central
S. C. FORSAITH MACHINE CO.
   foot West Auburn
Peter Harris. 17 Amherst

Charles H. Hutchinson Foundry and
   Machine Works, 327 to 371 Elm
Walter G. Jones, 1 Spring
Leighton Machine Co., East Freight
   Depot
J. A. V. Smith, Canal cor. West Brook
Benjamin F. Porter, 16 West Merrimack

Manufacturers.

American Card Clothing Co., card
   clothing. Canal, cor. West Brook
Burton Bros. baskets, 217 Manchester
William Corey Co., needles, 250 Concord cor. Maple
Dodge Needle Co., Canal East Freight
   Depot
Allen E. Eaton & Co.. tables, West
   Auburn
Emergency Fire Ex'inguishe. No. 92
   Manchester
S. C. FORSAITH MACHINE CO.,
   boxes, machinery, etc., foot West
   Auburn
Charles Noll, paper boxes, 423 Elm
John W. Mears, loom harness, Everett Knitting Works building
W. F. Moulton. eaves troughs, 650
   Elm
Manchester Locomotive Works, locomotives and fire engines, Canal,
   foot of Hollis
David B. Varney, brass foundry, 201
   Manchester
B. H. Piper Co., spokes, Beech St.,
   and P. R. R.
J. A. V. Smith, fliers, Electric Light
   building

Merchant Tailors.

Handy & Thayer, 827 Elm
Norman B. Hayes 852 Elm
William H. Mara, 15, 17 Manchester
ROBERT E. MCKEAN, 807 Elm
Plumer & Holton, 895 to 899 Elm
Elie Simard, 14 Amory
FRANK A. TILLMAN ,123 Hanover

Music and Musical Instruments.

E. T. Baldwin, The Kennard
Benjamin A. Bloomey, 240 Merrimack
Joseph S. Duggan, 961 Elm
WILLIAM H. ELLIOTT, 845 Elm
M. D. Fife & Co. 987 Elm
William F. Hart, 827 Elm
A. Z. Jenkins, The Kennard
Charles H. Kimball 73 Hanover
PIPER & MCINTIRE. 1059 Elm

Newspapers.

Mirror. Daily and Weekly, 64 Hanover
Deutscher Post. 30 Manchester
Emerald. 1118 Elm
L'Avenir National, 70 Merrimack

Manchester Advertiser, 141 Hanover
Manchester Union, Daily and Weekly
50 Hanover

Nickel and Silver Plating.

UNION MANUFACTURING CO.
near cor. Granite and Canal

Paper Manufacturers.

Amoskeag Paper Mills Co., Canal foot
West Brook
P. C. Cheney Co., Amoskeag

Passenger Agencies.

P. A. Devine, 100 Central
Herman Rodelsperger, 183 Douglas

Patent Solicitor.

JAMES B. THURSTON, 531 The Kennard

Patent Medicines.

BRAULT MEDICINE CO.
MCQUADE'S GENERAL STORE, 607
Elm

Photographers.

Whiting R. Call, 913 Elm
Lyman W. Colby, 20 Hanover
DESCLOS BROS, 70 West Central
Olivier Desmaris, 886 Elm
J. G. Ellinwood, 16 Patten block
J. T. LANGLEY, 780 Elm
Lindsey & Lecours, 987 Elm
Stephen Piper, 864 Elm
Sumner D. Quint, 939 Elm
HENRY C. WALLACE, 64 Hanover

Picture and Picture-Frame Manufacturers.

E. R. COBURN CO. 866 Elm
Hale & Whittemore, 978 Elm
Louis Manashewitz, 190 East Spruce
Miler & Obraztzoff, 124 Central
Temple & Farrington, 907, 909, 911
Elm

Plumbers and Gas Fitters.

Ashley A. Amlaw, 341 Pine
Arthur Belanger, 116 McGregor
A. L. Belanger, 116 McGregor
James A. Colby, 286 Merrimack
Michael A. Coleman, 374 Chestnut
Connor Bros, 49 Central
Garrett Cotter, 72 Spruce
William E. Goodwin 1172 Elm
David E. Guiney 649 Elm
Henry Horsfall, 50 Massabesic
Hovey & Spaulding 1030 Elm
Joseph B. Huneau & Son, 179 Manchester
Julian B. Huntley, 309 Concord

Thomas A Lane Co, 66 Hanover
John F. Larkin, 420 Cedar
MANCHESTER HEATING & LIGHTING Co. 1082 Elm
Theodore M. Miller & Co. 139 Concord
PIKE & HEALD CO. 972 Elm
Hervey Stratton, 20 South Main
C. LOUIS WOLF, 48 South Main

Printers.

Advertiser Publishing Co, 141 to 143
Hanover
Remy Bechard, 1056 Elm
A. S. Campbell & Co 21 Hanover
John B. Clarke Co, 64 Hanover
Deutscher Post, 30 Manchester
C. L. Fitzpatrick, 22 Concord
Fitzpatrick & Flood, Smyth block
Nate M. Kellogg Co. 970 Elm
LUSSIER BROS, 70 Merrimack
W. E. Moore, rear Opera House blk.
Novelty Advertising Co, 143 Hanover
T. H. Tuson 70 Manchester
J. ARTHUR WILLIAMS, 50 Manchester

Produce Dealers,—Wholesale.

Baker & Allen, 75 Granite
Burbank Bros, 303 Pine
B. FRANK WELCH, 3 to 7 Pleasant
DODGE & LAING, 20 Granite
James C. Furness 56 Granite
Gage & McDougall, Granite cor.
River
Alfred S. Lamb, 10 West Merrimack
Horace Marshall, 720 Elm
EDWARD M. SLAYTON CO, 64

Provisions,—Wholesale.

G. H. HAMMOND DRESSED BEEF
CO, 36 Granite
Manchester Beef Co, Franklin and
West Central
Manchester Provision Co, Cedar cor.
Franklin
Nelson Morris Co, 164 Franklin
E. M. SLAYTON CO, 64 Granite .
JOHE E. TOWLE & CO, 22 Granite

Real Estate Agents.

William C. Blodgett, 267 Lake ave.
HALBERT N. BOND, 340 The Kennard
George F. Bosher, 859 Elm
William A. Burgess, 913 Elm
Harry B. Cilley 1037 Elm
CLOUGH & TWOMBLEY, 886 Elm
G. A. Currier, 215 The Kennard
P. A. DEVINE, 100 Central
H. H. Dustin 924 Elm
William T. Evans, 385 Lake ave.
JAMES A. FOLSOM, Pembroke blk.
CHARLES C. HAYES, 339 The Kennard

A. J. Lane Co, $56 Elm
L. W. & A. A. Page, The Kennard
G. Allen Putnam, 121 Milford
John A. Sheehan 913 Elm
Frederick G. Stark, 236 South Main
Stark & Blanchet, 987 Elm
James G. Taggart, 64 Hanover
A. L. Walker & Son, 142 Merrimack

Roll Coverers.

Mrs. Charles B. Bradley, Stark Corp.,
  Spring

Roll Skin Manufacturers.

Kimball & Brown, 1168 Elm
J. E. Merrill & Co. 646 Elm

Sash, Doors, Blinds.

W. F. HUBBARD, Winter pl. 1368 Elm

Stamps for Collections.

FRANK C. LIVINGSTON, 859 Elm,
  room 7

Stencils and Rubber Stamps.

STAR STAMP CO, 6 Pleasant

Stoves, Ranges, Tinware, Etc.

Frank W. Blood Roofing Co. 397 Mer-
  rimack
James Briggs & Son, 714 Elm
W. A. Dakin & Co. 1054 Elm
A. DeMoulpied, 1105 Elm
CHARLES DeMOULPIED & Co. 23
  to 33 Lake ave.
NEW HAMPSHIRE FURNITURE
  STORE, The Kennard
MANCHESTER HEATING AND
  LIGHTING Co. 1682 Elm
Camille Marineau, 24 Pearl

Joseph J. Moreau, 55 Manchester
PIKE & HEALD Co. 972 Elm
Syndicate Furniture Co. 1097 Elm
G. R. Vance, 706 Elm
C. L. WOLF, 48 South Main

Tanners and Curriers.

Gerrish Wool and Leather Co. Brown
  ave.
Kimball & Brown, rear 1168 Elm
J. E. Merrill & Co. 646 Elm

Trunk Manufacturers.

J. TRUESDALE & SON, 579 Elm
N. J. WHALEN, 1110 Elm and 97 to
  101 Merrimack

Undertakers.

F. X. Chenette, 382 Chestnut
Thomas F. Collins, 104 Central
FRANK L. GRAY, 1088 Elm
Kean & Sheehan, 68 Merrimack
Pierre Lemieau, 30 Bridge
ALFRED E. MORSE, 4 and 5 Stark
Royal D. Sleeper, 357 East Spruce
E. V. Turcotte, 196 Manchester
F. L. WALLACE & CO, 55 Hanover

Variety Stores.

A. Benjamine, 28 Amherst
G. F. Bowen & Co. 332 Granite
S. E. Butterfield, 1303 Elm
Mrs. K. Clancy, 500 Elm
Joseph Demers & Co. 150 to 154
  McGregor
B. E. Fernald, 47 Massabesic
Miss Lizzie Gillis, 1199 Elm
Roscoe K. Horne, 826 to 832 Elm
F. E. Nelson, 928 Elm
J. J. Stanton, 110 Central
F. W. Woolworth & Co. 985 Elm

WHAT IS AN "AD-SMITH"?

An "Ad-Smith" is a man who writes advertisements for
those too busy to write their own, and who undertakes to keep
ones business announcements up to date. That is my business. Do you need me? If so, address me at the Board of
Trade rooms, and I think we can arrange terms satisfactory to
all concerned.

FRANK H. CHALLIS.

MANCHESTER BOARD OF TRADE.

Organized February 5, 1890.

For the promotion of the prosperity of the Queen City of New Hampshire.

HEADQUARTERS IN THE KENNARD.

OFFICERS OF THE BOARD FOR 1896.

CHARLES H. BARTLETT, *President.*

W. G. AFRICA, O. D. KNOX, *Vice-Presidents.*

HENRY CHANDLER, *Treasurer.*

HERBERT W. EASTMAN, *Secretary.*

DIRECTORS.

Charles H. Bartlett, William E. Drew, Frank Preston, Ernest C. Wescott, Nicholas J. Whalen, Albert L. Clough, Clarence M. Edgerly, Frank L. Way, Eugene Quirin.

COMMITTEES FOR 1896.

On Finance — E. C. Wescott, E. W. Perkins, Joseph Quirin, L. H. Gould, H. F. W. Little.

On Manufacturing and Mercantile Affairs — N. J. Whalen, J. B. Estey, F. C. Miville, D. M. Poore, H. N. Bond.

On Municipal Affairs — Albert L. Clough, N. P. Hunt, John C. French, J. J. Abbott, L. P. Reynolds.

On Insurance — Clarence M. Edgerly, John J. Dillon, W. H. Goggin, W. S. Martin, Jr., George Blanchet.

On Railroads and Transportation — William E. Drew, A. C. Wallace, James F. Cavanaugh, E. H. Carroll, Edward Wagner.

On New Enterprises and Industries — Frank Preston, William Corey, Edwin Kennedy, S. H. Mead, C. L. Wolf.

On Statistics — Frank L. Way, Joseph Kidder, William E. Moore, Arthur T. Beaumier, J. A. Sheehan.

THE QUEEN CITY JOURNAL.

PUBLISHED QUARTERLY BY HERBERT W. EASTMAN.

A handsomely printed and illustrated Journal, devoted to the business interests of Manchester in particular and New Hampshire in general.

Sent to any address for 50 Cents a Year.

82

PINK TONIC!

In offering this preparation to the public, we are pushing no quack nostrum, but a regular physician's prescription which has met with remarkable success in giving tone to the system, regulating the liver, and giving it a healthy action.

The liver is one of the most important organs of the body; on its health depends the health of the whole internal system.

Now, then, it is plain to be seen that it is just as impossible for the blood to be in a pure state, with the liver in an unhealthy condition, as it is impossible to have impure blood when the liver is in perfect working order.

When the liver is torpid or sluggish and a person is in the condition known as Bilious, the system is ripe to take on any contagious disease.

Disease Cannot Exist Before This Conqueror!

In cases of constipation the result will be greatly hastened by taking our **Pink Alterative Powder** in connection with **Pink Tonic.**

Price of PINK TONIC, 75 Cents.
Price of PINK ALTERATIVE POWDER, 25 Cents.

If your druggist will not supply you, send to

SNELLING & WOODS,

Proprietors,

1167 Elm St., cor. Bridge, Manchester, N. H.

Reliable Testimonials furnished at our office.

ÆT THE FIRST ALARM ILLNESS

MAKE A RUN FOR

LOCATION OF FIRE ALARM BOXES.

3	Blood's Lower Shop	45	Forsaith Machine Shop
4	Spruce and Elm	51	Walker and Second
5	Merrimack and Elm	52	Barr's Block, 'Squog
6	City Hall	53	Main and Mast
7	Police Station	54	A and Bowman
8	Elm and Hollis	56	Mast Road, near Riddle
9	Elm and Webster	61	River Road and Hancock
12	North and Pine	62	Gerrish's Tannery
13	Brook and Chestnut	71	Cedar and Pine
14	Prospect and Union	72	Lake Avenue and Lincoln
15	Pearl and Chestnut	73	Beech and Cedar
16	Lowell and Union	81	Central Station, Vine St.
17	Amherst and Beech	82	Lowell and Elm back St.
18	Manchester and Maple	112	Sagamore and Union
21	Merrimack and Pine	113	Oak and Prospect
23	Central and Beech	114	Pearl and Ash
24	Massabesic and Lake Avenue	212	Shoe Shop, Hallsville
25	Hanover and Ashland	213	Beech St. and P. R. R.
26	Bridge and Russell	214	Elliott Silk Mill
27	Belmont and Amherst	215	Hoyt's Shoe Shop
31	Canal and Hollis	261	Pearl St. Grammar School
32	Canal and Brook	312	Putnam and Main
34	Jefferson Mill	313	Amory and Main
35	Stark Mills	314	Cheney's Paper Mill
36	Amory Mills	315	Old Brick Store, 'Skeag
39	County Jail	321	Beauport and Wayne
41	Amoskeag Mills	323	Putnam and Bartlett
42	Manchester Mills	511	Douglass and Green
43	Olzendam's Mills	513	Milford, near Carroll

Out-of-Town Calls, 2-2-2. All Out Signal, two blows on the bell. Test Signal, one blow, 12.30, noon. **Military Call,** twelve blows, twice. School Signals, 1-1 closes primary and middle schools; 2-2 closes all schools; given at 7.45, 11.30 A. M., or 1.15 P. M.

INDEX.

84

WHAT is so much to be desired, amid the changes of fortune, the fluctuations of health, incapacitating sicknesses of life, and the feebleness of age as a fixed and certain income; an income whose amount is known in advance and the certainty of its being paid you on a certain day is absolute.

Amid doubt and fear, the loss of fortune and friends, girt by perils seen and unseen, in the agony of swift sickness, in the growing feebleness of age, what so blessed as to know that for you and those you love there is laid by, accumulating, held in reserve, a sure and ample provision for every actual need of life even to life's latest day.

It is just here, at this point of view, that the mind of one who has money to invest for his children, for his dependents, for charity or for himself in his advancing years, receives its illumination. For if he be intelligent he knows only too well how unsatisfactory, because uncertain, are the processes provided by law or sanctified by custom among us Americans, for the transmission not of property but of income-earning investments from one generation to another.

How shall the wife, unaccustomed to business, be surely provided for or protected against her own inexperience? How shall the children, in case of sudden death of the father, be still the recipients of his loving care and prescience? How shall the aging parents, as the riskful years multiply, have a sure and ample provision made for them? And how shall he himself, the man in his vigorous prime, chief motor at the centre of large affairs, securely armor himself against the slings and arrows of outrageous fortune that may at any time assault him and leave him battered, bruised and prostrate on the field of financial defeat?

These are interrogations which intelligent men in all branches of business and walks of life are trying to answer, and are finding answers satisfactory to themselves in the methods of investment provided for them by the Mutual Life Insurance Company of New York, as its daily record of increasing business in the direction of annuities testifies.

ADDRESS BY W. H. H. MURRAY.

The Mutual Life celebrated its Semi-Centennial three years earlier than Manchester, and during its entire existence its bonds have never been quoted below par, or discounted by the fraction of a cent. It is and has long been the largest and strongest monetary corporation on earth. Its assets today exceed $220,000,000 — more than three times the combined deposits of all the savings banks of New Hampshire. It paid to policy holders in 1895 above $23,000,000, and since organization has returned over $411,000,000. The ablest financiers are among its patrons and YOU are invited to call at our office and investigate its many attractive investment policies.

Amoskeag Savings Bank.

Persons seeking a safe depository for their surplus funds will deposit them in the Amoskeag Savings Bank, where they will have the benefit of the

$250,000 GUARANTY FUND.

To protect them against loss, and receive a fair rate of interest free from taxes.

Deposits go on interest the first day of every month.

MOODY CURRIER,

President.

HENRY CHANDLER,

Treasurer.